T0273333

THE
ENVISION
METHOD[SM]

THE
ENVISION
METHOD[SM]

HOW SMART WOMEN
GET SAVVY ABOUT MONEY

LINDSEY McKAY

Published by Advantage, Charleston, South Carolina.
Member of Advantage Media Group.

ADVANTAGE is a registered trademark, and the Advantage colophon is a trademark of Advantage Media Group, Inc.

Printed in the United States of America.

10 9 8 7 6 5 4 3 2 1

ISBN: 978-1-64225-137-1
LCCN: 2022910746

Cover design by Josh Frederick.
Layout design by Mary Hamilton.

This publication is designed to provide accurate and authoritative information in regard to the subject matter covered. It is sold with the understanding that the publisher is not engaged in rendering legal, accounting, or other professional services. If legal advice or other expert assistance is required, the services of a competent professional person should be sought.

Advantage Media Group is a publisher of business, self-improvement, and professional development books and online learning. We help entrepreneurs, business leaders, and professionals share their Stories, Passion, and Knowledge to help others Learn & Grow. Do you have a manuscript or book idea that you would like us to consider for publishing? Please visit **advantagefamily.com**.

To Sloane, Emerson, and Sawyer.
Always be empowered and confident on your journey
to a purpose-filled life!

CONTENTS

INTRODUCTION
MONEY MEMORIES

What is money? Money is defined as a medium of exchange, a form of payment, a measure of value. We are taught to think of money as a commodity, the cash in our purse or the balance in our bank account. But that's just the economics of it; money is about so much more than dollars and cents.

Your financial decisions are likely driven more by the feelings you associate with money than by facts, figures, and goals. The way you feel about money and the emotions it evokes are as unique as you are. Your early experiences carry significant weight and are likely the foundation of your financial beliefs. It might be the happiness that buying something gave you—the sense of accomplishment in working hard and being rewarded. Or it may be the sense of fear and lack of security you experienced from not having access to money. As life goes on, you continue to have new experiences with money that result in lasting memories. These memories may reinforce your earlier feelings, or they may alter your views.

Your money memories translate to your money mindset, and this subconscious mindset drives financial decision-making. Understanding the root of your behavior will enable you to take control of your finances with the same confidence and enthusiasm that you approach the rest of your life with. I aspire to help all you smart, talented, successful women be empowered by your money mindset and forever approach financial decision-making from a position of knowledge and strength.

Like many of you, my own personal history set the foundation for my money mindset. My father was a financial advisor and a major influence on my money memories. It was important to him that I understood money from an early age. He's the type of father (and now grandfather) that views *everything* as an opportunity to teach a life lesson. When it came to money, that didn't just mean the mechanics of spending and saving but understanding how to use money as a tool in life.

I learned that money must be earned. I learned the importance of saving for larger, more meaningful purchases rather than spending all my allowance on candy or video games. And when I asked for an advance on my allowance, I learned the finer points of paying interest as a consequence of borrowing money I had not yet earned.

After starting my first job, I learned how much of my paycheck I could spend versus the amount I should save for future rainy days. When I started driving, I learned the importance of insurance and, later, how much rates can increase after even a small fender bender. When I decided to attend New York University, I learned the difference between in-state and private tuition costs and how student loans could help me afford the latter.

At times it felt like some of these lessons were learned the hard way, but now, as an adult, I appreciate how my father used real-life moments to teach me about money. I was taught to put a greater emphasis on the importance of good financial decisions in everyday life.

Early life lessons also incorporated understanding the difference between wanting and needing. I was fortunate to have a middle-class suburban upbringing. I had the luxury of wanting things that I did not need. If my sisters or I told our father that we wanted a new toy or a bike, he would ask us, "How does it feel to want?" His message: Be thankful for having all that you need; if you concentrate only on what you do not have, you will never have enough.

We learned to pay that gratitude forward, seeking out ways to support our community. We volunteered at soup kitchens, adopted families at the holidays, and helped recently immigrated families become established in our neighborhood. I can't say that I realized how deep an impact it made at the time, but it left an imprint on all of us. Not only did we learn the distinction between necessity and desire, but it also instilled a passion to be of service to others.

While my desire to be of service ultimately led me to become a financial planner, another money memory drives my commitment to helping women gain confidence in their financial futures. I grew up in a traditional household where my father was the breadwinner, and my mother was responsible for running the household. Every family dynamic looks different, but, like many couples, my parents separated household and financial responsibilities. This worked well for our family until my parents parted ways and the division of duties was disrupted. We all had to take on new roles, and for my mother that meant reestablishing her career after eighteen years outside the workforce.

For the next twenty-five years, my mother strove to create financial empowerment. She dutifully worked for a single employer, allowing her to accrue a pension. Rather than selling a property that she received in her divorce settlement, she maintained it as a rental property and eventually remodeled it to create space where she could live while earning income by renting out the other half of the house.

She recently sold that property, purchased a single-family rambler, and even set some money aside as part of her reserve funds for retirement. When the time came for her to retire, she told me, "I feel more secure now than ever before." Both as a financial advisor and as a daughter, I am proud of all that she has done to be at a point where she feels in control of her financial future.

Being capable of controlling your financial future is the definition of **financial empowerment**. This does not mean having enough money to never work again, although it could. It means being in the position to create options and make decisions that allow you to control your own destiny.

> **BEING CAPABLE OF CONTROLLING YOUR FINANCIAL FUTURE IS THE DEFINITION OF FINANCIAL EMPOWERMENT.**

Like your personal history, your definition of financial empowerment is unique to you. Financial empowerment is about what you want your money to enable *you* to do. My own experiences have led me to correlate empowerment with maintaining independence: being responsible for earning *and* managing my own money. However you define empowerment, it's about being intentional in creating the capacity for choice. That could mean the ability to work part time or stay at home full time. It could mean the option to make a major career change or start your own business. It could mean the ability to travel for extended periods of time or choosing to live where you are the happiest. Choices enable you to be adaptable, and that flexibility will give you greater control of your financial future.

In *The ENVISION Method*, I will help you identify your money mindset, define what financial empowerment means to you, and show you how to create a plan to achieve it.[1] Having a plan is the start of your journey, as you know life will give you a lot to conquer along the way. To illustrate the real-life ups and downs you may face, we will follow the stories of three different women, Elle, Collins, and Jade, as they navigate life with their finances in mind. I hope that through their stories you will see slivers of yourself, learn from their experiences, and gain confidence in your own approach to finding financial empowerment.

I know that outlining your hopes and dreams can be daunting, and looking in the mirror can be intimidating. This is hard for me, too—and I'm an expert! The willingness to take risks is hard, but the more you know, the better you'll feel about making financial decisions that will allow you to define your future. When you have the knowledge and confidence to take control of your finances, you will

- be more inclined to create and stick to a plan,

- improve your financial decision-making,

- be prepared for unexpected life events,

- gain confidence in investing, and

- be in control of your financial future!

PART I

MEET OUR INVESTORS

Meet Elle, Collins, and Jade.[2] I have labeled them *investors* to acknowledge that the work we put into financial empowerment is an investment in ourselves. Having met in college and now being in their late thirties, their friendship spans over twenty years. They have studied together, traveled together, and supported each other through major life changes. Once a month, no matter what is going on in their lives, they meet to catch up on life and discuss the important stuff—children, careers, relationships, health, and even finances. Together they learn and lean on each other to navigate all that life brings.

While their lives have become interwoven, their personalities and money mindsets remain uniquely their own.

ELLE

Elle has a very head-down, functional relationship with money, having grown up in a home where money was scarce. The only conversations about money she heard growing up were arguments about whether her family would have enough to pay the bills. Even though years have passed since Elle saw debt collectors show up at her parents' house, those memories will never leave her.

Her money memories of scarcity have led her to be a diligent saver. She is hesitant to spend money outside of necessity, spending on needs only, never indulging in things she wants. Being antidebt, Elle made her way through college with financial aid and part-time work. To this day she is so worried about not having enough money, she never buys anything she cannot afford and prefers to pay for everything with cash.

Elle's unexpected divorce at age thirty-two left her the single mother of a now-eight-year-old daughter, Ava. Managing a single-income household reinforced her mindset of feeling like she will never have enough. To create more financial security, she works two jobs, a full-time job at a local nonprofit and a part-time job as a cycle instructor.

Elle's money mindset is rooted in survival and self-reliance.

COLLINS

If you ask Collins what her approach to money is, she will say, "I know how to spend it!" Unlike Elle, Collins has never had to think about money. She grew up in an affluent home and finished college without any debt thanks to financial support from her family. Collins got married at twenty-five to her college sweetheart, James, and bought their first home with a down payment gifted to them by her parents. James's income provides a comfortable lifestyle for their family of four, allowing Collins to step away from her high-powered career after welcoming their second child.

Collins and James have a divide and conquer approach to their household, with James responsible for paying the bills and managing the finances while Collins focuses on caring for the children and the upkeep of their home. Collins finds these roles to be agreeable and is grateful for the lifestyle this affords.

Collins's money mindset is one of free-spirited abundance.

JADE

Jade is the youngest of five children. While her upbringing was loving, each of the kids in her family was expected to be responsible and somewhat self-sufficient—keeping track of five kids was a challenge! Because of this, Jade learned how to spend and save from her older siblings. By observing them stretch money from allowances, birthdays, and odd jobs, Jade learned that if managed well, money can provide extras.

Having paid for college using student loans, Jade understands how borrowing money can enable her to achieve otherwise unobtainable goals. Her willingness to borrow led her to become a homeowner at an early age. As a corporate accountant, Jade believes in working hard and paying herself first before indulging in life's extras. While she isn't married, she lives with her partner of thirteen years, Logan. Jade and Logan have a "mine" and "yours" approach to finances, keeping their assets completely separate, including Jade's house, which she maintains as a rental property.

Jade's money mindset is practicality with a hint of opportunism.

CHAPTER ONE
SMART DREAMS

July

At the beginning of every year, Elle, Collins, and Jade set goals so they can encourage each other's success, help hold each other accountable for their outcomes, and celebrate their accomplishments. Together they have conquered everything from dating to detoxing. And this year, with their lives and careers continuing to become more established, they each promised to get their financial circumstances in order. Unlike when it came to their past goal-setting sessions, they have struggled for months to jump-start progress on their financial goals.

Jade, always the first to take charge, drops a pile of magazines on the coffee table in Collins's living room. The women each pick up a pair of scissors and an assortment of magazines, with the purpose of crafting vision boards for what they want their lives to look like in the future. They add pictures that include families, houses, cars, and beautiful, secluded turquoise beaches. The intention behind the vision boards that Elle, Collins, and Jade are creating is to envision a future in which they can imagine themselves, dreaming of all that is possible. They will use that world, and the emotions that it invokes, to lay the groundwork for setting their financial goals.

Collins looks up from her own vision board of designer brands, luxury cars, tropical beaches, and mountain resorts and glances around the table at the progress the other women have made.

Seeing a University of Washington logo, Collins asks if Elle plans to go back to school. "I wish I had the time to get another degree. This is about saving for Ava. I would like to be able to pay for her education," Elle answers, shrinking as she thinks of the meager balance in Ava's savings account.

Jade spreads out a few houses and a number—fifty-five. "I want to buy another rental property with Logan to help support our income in retirement," Jade says as she imagines herself and Logan retiring early, at the age of fifty-five.

Elle, too, has cut out pictures of houses. For Elle purchasing a home represents the security and stability that she longs to provide for her daughter.

With much excitement Collins shares the colorful and extravagant pictures she has cut out. "Your board looks like you're already retired." Jade laughs as she momentarily fantasizes about traveling during her retirement years.

Collins suggests that Jade's board could benefit from the addition of some color. "Your board is all about retirement, but what about life before you retire?" she asks Jade.

"Maybe you're right," Jade says, reaching for the copy of *Travel + Leisure*. As she flips through the glossy pages filled with gorgeous backdrops and exquisite resorts, her thoughts are stuck on Collins's comment. What is at the root of her tunnel vision for getting to retirement?

WHERE ARE YOU COMING FROM?

Before you work on where you want to go, it's important to know where you are coming from. Take a moment to reflect on the life experiences that have shaped your money mindset. Our ideas about money are formulated from such a young age that we do not always recognize where they come from. However, understanding your past experiences with money can help you recognize how you have been conditioned to view money.

We see the way our investors feel about money reflected in their vision boards. Having grown up in a household where money was scarce, Elle's money memories have caused her to fear that she will never have a sense of financial security. Her goals are driven by her desire to provide for her daughter. She is diligent about saving but still lacks confidence in her ability to achieve her goals. At the other end of the spectrum, Collins is overconfident about her ability to afford the finer things in life. Having never had to think much about money, she's not afraid to spend it and does not worry about how her family will be provided for. Falling in the middle, Jade is not afraid of not having enough and will forgo current splurges (shopping, travel, etc.) in order to make progress toward her long-term goal of retiring early.

How have your memories affected your relationship with money—how you spend, save, and invest? Moncy may be a source of fear or strength, just like it may conjure up good or bad memories. As you examine your history with money, write down the feelings and emotions associated with it. How do you characterize your money mindset?

Elle's money mindset continues to be filled with anxiety. She acknowledges that this has, at times, prevented her from being able to make financial decisions. Being single and solely responsible for decision-making compounds her feeling of insecurity. Collins admittedly does not have a healthy money mindset. There is a disconnect for her between spending and saving, her approach being "If you have it, spend it." Money having always been readily available to her, Collins tends not to attach emotion to it. Jade's mindset is to use money as a tool for advancement. While Jade is practical, she also looks for opportunities to leverage her money to do more for her. She is proud of the early financial decisions that she has made and continues to be focused on making good decisions for her early retirement.

What, if anything, would you like to change about your money mindset? How can you work to acknowledge the emotions and ensure that they do not override your planning? It's not easy to let the emotions go, but recognizing what you want to change is the first step. Now is the time to acknowledge the need to reform any bad habits and take charge of your own financial narrative.

WHAT, IF ANYTHING, WOULD YOU LIKE TO CHANGE ABOUT YOUR MONEY MINDSET? HOW CAN YOU WORK TO ACKNOWLEDGE THE EMOTIONS AND ENSURE THAT THEY DO NOT OVERRIDE YOUR PLANNING?

Excited about their commitment to helping each other, Elle aspires to conquer her self-limiting beliefs by learning how to improve her financial circumstances. Collins is less enthusiastic about her agreement to be more intentional when it comes to financial matters. Seeing the boards that Elle and Jade made has opened her eyes to how differently they are thinking about their financial futures. She feels uneasy admitting how little she is engaged in her personal finances. Jade wonders if she needs to work on finding better balance between saving for tomorrow and living for today. Jade feels most confident when she has a plan. The vision-board exercise caused her to take pause, creating an opportunity for her to affirm that her plan is on the right track and identify any gaps that she may have overlooked.

WHERE DO YOU WANT TO GO?

Now that you have a better understanding of what shaped your relationship with money, you can better define what financial empowerment means to you. Phrases like *financial empowerment* and *financial independence* are often tossed around without any substantive definition connected to them, which is why in the introduction I intentionally defined financial empowerment as *being in a position to create options and make decisions that allow you to control your financial future.*

Think of financial empowerment as your personal financial vision statement. You work hard; what are the things that you want that money to be able to help you achieve? What does financial confidence look like for you? It should encompass not only *what* you want to achieve but *why* it is important to you.

It could be providing security for your family by not having to worry about living paycheck to paycheck. It could be living a stress-free financial life by eliminating all your debt. It could mean decreasing your anxiety by being engaged in your family's finances. It could mean managing the aspects of your financial life to take charge of your own future. It could mean becoming so confident in your financial security that you have the capacity to start something brand new.

For Elle financial empowerment is providing security to her family. She longs to provide stability for her daughter by buying a home and being able to pay for Ava's education. Collins wants to be knowledgeable about their family's financial circumstances through a passive role. She wishes to maintain her carefree lifestyle while being assured that she truly does not have to worry. For Jade early retirement is the ultimate measure of a successful career, and she aims to be confident in achieving that level of success. She aspires to support herself without having to work nine to five when she's fifty-five.

Knowing your why is an essential step in the process of identifying meaningful financial goals. Your definition of financial empowerment may evolve over time, but it is important to start by identifying what you are striving to achieve. Once you have clarity around where you want to go, you can outline the steps that you need to take to get there.

CREATE SMART GOALS

Financial goal setting is vital to achieving the big vision you have for your life. According to a study by Leadership IQ on the gender gap and goal setting, people who explicitly describe or envision their goals are anywhere from 1.2 to 1.4 times more likely to successfully accomplish their goals.[3] This is just one of numerous studies that point to the power of bringing your goals out of your head and putting them on paper—either by writing them out or using pictures. This can be done in every aspect of your life, including your journey to financial empowerment.

Our investors will only realize the dreams and desires on their vision boards if they have the financial capacity to make them happen. Having identified what they want to achieve, they will now work to further define their goals. Outlining SMART goals will help to focus their efforts and further increase their chance of success.

Specific: Clearly defined without ambiguity

Measurable: Have trackable metrics

Achievable: Attainable and realistic

Relevant: Align with vision of financial empowerment

Timely: Include a clear timeline

BE SPECIFIC

Goals that are well defined have a significantly greater chance of being accomplished. The more specific your goal, the more you'll understand the steps necessary to achieve it. The best way to make a goal more specific is to consider the four Ws—why, what, who, and when. Let's break down the Ws of our investors' goals.

Elle's goals: **Why does she want to achieve her goals?** She wants to create stability and security for her daughter's future. **What does she want to accomplish?** Create a home of their own and help Ava receive an education. **Who is involved?** Elle and Ava. **When does she want to achieve these goals?** Ava's age drives both of her timelines. She has ten years until Ava begins college and a five-year target for her home purchase.

Jade's goals also address all the Ws. **Why:** To enjoy early retirement free of financial worry. **What:** Purchase a rental property and retire at fifty-five. **Who:** Jade and Logan. **When:** Five years (rental) and seventeen years (retirement).

Collins's goals are not as specific. She wants to buy a new car and take annual family vacations. While she knows a few of her Ws, she realizes that she will need to spend more time narrowing her focus.

SET METRICS

While Collins works to make her goals more specific, Elle and Jade move on to determining how to quantify their goals, making them measurable. **How much money do they need to save** for college and retirement? How much house can they afford? **How will they track their progress toward their goals?** Will they monitor their progress monthly, quarterly, or annually? **How will they know they have reached their goal?** Is the primary driver dollars or time? If their goal is reached ahead of their timeline, do they stop saving?

Elle estimates in-state tuition costs of $10,000 per year and sets Ava's education goal as $40,000. Using her father's advice, Jade sets a target of $1 million in retirement savings. Identifying savings goals for their real estate purchases is not as straightforward. There are multiple factors that will determine the ranges for their purchase price. They decide to narrow their focus to saving for their down payments. Elle sets a goal of $70,000, and Jade sets a goal of $30,000. Both establish monthly savings goals and will monitor their progress every six months. Their goals of retirement and college will be completed when the milestone occurs, making these goals time driven, while their down payment goals will be reached when they achieve their specified dollar amount.

> **EMPOWER TIP:** Track your goal progress every six months and reevaluate as needed. If you find that you are on track, reward yourself in small but meaningful ways!

ACHIEVABLE

Goals should always be realistic to ensure that they are attainable within the desired time frame. In the next chapter, we will see our investors dive into their finances to determine their ability to achieve their goals. **How can they accomplish their goals?** Do they have enough income to save for their goals? **Are their goals reachable given their resources and timeline?** Are there other actions that would put them in a better position to work toward their goals? **Are they committed to achieving their goals**?

RELEVANT TO DREAMS

One way to ensure their commitment is to focus on goals that support their financial empowerment. Personal definitions of financial empowerment make it easy for our investors to align their goals with what matters most to them. In determining the relevance of their goals, they will want to consider the following: **How will this contribute to their financial empowerment?** How will this goal help build on their other goals? **Is now the right time to set this goal?** Will this goal detract resources from other goals or obligations?

TIMELINE TO SUCCESS

Although many women think they must choose between improving the quality of their daily lives or bettering their finances over the longer term, these two do not need to be mutually exclusive. Setting short-, mid-, and long-term goals will create a road map of how you can accomplish both and everything in between.

    Short-term goals are the best place to start in your financial goal setting. Short-term goals are things that you want to accomplish as quickly as possible, such as establishing emergency savings, reducing debt, or maximizing your retirement contributions. Short-term goals generally involve a smaller dollar amount, making them easier to achieve in a targeted time frame, typically less than three years. The path to achieving these goals is clear, and you know every step you need to take to do it.

SHORT-TERM GOALS:

Motivate and energize you. Having a shorter time period makes it easier to track and see your progress, which positively reinforces your behavior.

Help solve future money problems. Setting short-term goals to save for large expenditures can prevent you from depending on short-term borrowing in the future.

Midterm goals are slightly larger in dollar amount than short-term goals and therefore take longer to achieve. The amount of time it takes to achieve these goals may not be as clear cut. These goals typically span three to ten years and for many people are harder to identify. Some examples include planning for a major home renovation, building a college fund, or paying off a large debt, like student or auto loans. These goals should help you make progress toward your long-term goals. Accomplishing them gets you one step closer to the life you envision. They encompass both the small and big things that impact the trajectory of your future.

MIDTERM GOALS:

Focus your attention once your short-term goals have been achieved. You are already in the habit of saving; continue with that intention.

Act as stepping-stones, setting you up for long-term financial success. Focus on goals that will increase your net worth over time.

Long-term goals are ten years out or further. These include retiring, paying off your mortgage, and making sure your parents are taken care of. For many of us, they seem so far in the future that we frequently put off planning or saving for them, believing that we will find money for them later. But the earlier you start, the better off you will be. Think of long-term goals as all your other goals coming together. When everything falls into place, what does your ideal life look like?

LONG-TERM GOALS:

Focus on the big picture. Financial empowerment, or the freedom to make choices, is greater when you have a solid foundation to build on.

Increase your motivation and persistence. Achieving your short- and midterm goals should contribute to the success of your long-term goals.

Benefit from time. These types of goals typically require larger dollar amounts. The earlier you start planning and saving for them, the longer you have to build up the funds needed.

As our investors outline their SMART goals, we once again see how money mindsets can subconsciously impact our financial focus. Elle and Collins, and to some extent Jade, note that they have clustered their goals around a specific segment in their timelines.

	ELLE	COLLINS	JADE
Dream	First house	New car	Investment property
Goal	$70,000	$40,000	$30,000
Timeline	5 years Midterm	2 years Short-term	5 years Midterm
Dream	Ava's education	Dream family vacation	Early retirement
Goal	$40,000	$15,000	$1 million
Timeline	10 years Midterm	1 year Short-term	17 years Long-term

Elle's goals revolve around her daughter, tilting them to the next ten years, before Ava starts college. While Ava will always be her top priority, Elle should consider what she wants in the near term as well as the long term.

Collins, not one to concern herself with the future, has identified only immediate, material goals. She realizes that it if she is going to work to be more intentional with her money, she will need to set more meaningful goals that look beyond the next year or two.

Finally, Jade's tunnel vision causes her to overlook goals that she may have outside of supporting her retirement. Retiring early is an important goal for Jade, but she could be missing out on current opportunities in life.

EMPOWER TIP: Set short-, mid-, and long-term goals, allowing your goals to build on themselves and creating a clear timeline for your financial success!

YOUR GOALS DON'T HAVE TO BE SET IN STONE

Just as our investors are discovering, you may find that you want to add new goals or change your goals as you further define them. Financial goals can be revised at any time, for any reason. As you gain a better understanding of your finances, you may want to revisit your goals. And as your life changes, you will need to adapt your financial goals. If you experience a stumbling block, you can always pause and take a step back. You may have to adjust your current plan or create a new plan to get you through tough times. At any time, you can work to get back on track or decide that new goals would better serve you.

FINANCIAL GOALS CAN BE REVISED AT ANY TIME, FOR ANY REASON.

Similarly, if a life event positively impacts your finances, you should revisit and refine your goals.

That's the beauty of setting and tracking goals: you can make changes as your circumstances change or as your dreams evolve. The important thing is to establish a strong foundation to support your financial empowerment. While it may take some time, you will start to see even the little steps creating change, allowing you to make more confident choices and live the financial life you want.

> **EMPOWER TIP:** As our investors have, share your goals with others. This solidifies your commitment to your goals, creates accountability, and gets other people invested in your success!

TAKE ACTION!

Throughout the book, you can use the ENVISION Method to guide you in your pursuit of financial empowerment. Before moving on to strategies that will help you achieve and protect your financial goals, I encourage you to begin to **ENVISION** your future.

E   **EMPOWER** yourself by letting go of the past and dream of the life that you want to have!

N   **NARROW** your focus by creating SMART goals that align with your vision of financial empowerment.

V   **VALIDATE** your ability to achieve your goals, ensuring that your goals are realistic.

I   **IMPLEMENT** your plan by taking action today! Use short-, mid-, and long-term goals as building blocks.

S   **SHARE** your goals with others to keep you committed and accountable.

I   **INCENTIVIZE** yourself to stay motivated and engaged by celebrating milestones.

O   **OVERSEE** your progress, monitoring every six months to start and at least annually after.

N   **NAVIGATE** life along the way, reviewing and revising your goals as needed.

CHAPTER TWO

WHERE THE
MONEY GOES

August

Elle and Jade are enjoying the late-day sun in Jade's backyard as they wait for Collins to join them for their monthly meetup.

"How has Ava's summer been?" Jade asks Elle.

"Great. You know that girl; she wants to go to every camp there is. I don't even know how she finds all of them," Elle says with bewilderment. "She wanted to go to a robotics and animation camp, and I had to tell her no because it cost too much. As she gets older, her interests are getting more and more expensive."

"Just wait until she becomes a teenager," Jade says sympathetically.

"I guess I shouldn't be complaining. I should be thankful that she's interested in STEM camps. But I do miss the days when she was content at the community center." Elle sighs with a reminiscent tone.

"How much do summer camps run these days?" inquires Jade.

"Most are between $300 and $500 per week. The one that I said no to was $700," Elle says.

"Wow, you are spending as much as $5,000 a summer on camps?" Jade says, blown away.

"Childcare isn't cheap. Why do you think I have an additional part-time job?" Elle says, half joking.

"I know it's a big expense. I guess I just never really looked at the numbers," Jade admits, a bit embarrassed.

Elle laughs. "Just think how much money you are saving by not having kids."

"I once heard that the cost of raising a child is over $265,000, and that did not include the cost of college,"[4] Jade says, recalling a recent article she read.

"So you have looked at the numbers," Elle says with a smile.

"It didn't fully register at the time," Jade admits and then remembers: "One of your financial goals is Ava's college savings. How much did you estimate that will be?"

"The cost keeps going up! I actually looked again when we set our goals, and it will be at least $40,000. I have $10,000," Elle says, crestfallen.

"She's only eight. You have plenty of time," Jade reassures her.

"At this rate I will be at half of that," Elle states in frustration. "I am saving as much as I can. I feel like it's never going to be enough," she says quietly, trailing off in self-doubt.

"That's why we are working on it. We will come up with a plan to make it happen." Jade states this with so much confidence that Elle finds herself believing it.

Many of us feel like Elle. How do you know that you are saving enough? Goal setting identifies the areas where you want to save, and the next step is determining how much you can afford to save. These are the metrics that make your goals measurable. Once you know how much you can put aside, you can prioritize how to allocate the savings to your goals, set the timeline to achieving them, and track your progress along the way.

KNOW WHAT YOU TAKE HOME

This may sound obvious, but the first step in knowing how much to save is knowing what you earn. We will focus on after-tax income, but now is a good time to take a look at your full benefits picture. Do you receive additional benefits, such as health insurance, an employer-sponsored retirement plan, and life or disability insurance? Are you taking full advantage of these and any other benefits offered by your employer? Make sure you are maximizing all that is available to you and that your compensation is commensurate with your role and experience.

Let's look at each of our investors' annual *after-tax* incomes, as they will use those, as well as the goals they set in the last chapter, to establish their spending and saving habits.

Elle: $60,000, including $10,000 from her part-time job

Collins: $300,000 household income, earned by James

Jade: $100,000, plus $20,000 rental-property income*

*Both are individual incomes separate from Logan.

THE 50/20/30 RULE

While you likely already know how much money you make, do you know where all the money goes? We don't always track our spending very closely; we simply make sure that we have enough coming in to cover the amount that goes out. And as our income increases, our spending seems to increase right along with it. But how much of what you spend is driven by everyday needs, and how much of it goes to things that you don't necessarily need but want?

The 50/20/30 rule is a practical and effective framework for how to allocate your income, placing your money into three categories:

Everyday essentials = 50 percent

Goals and reserves = 20 percent

Lifestyle = 30 percent

EVERYDAY ESSENTIALS

Start by determining the expenses that cover your daily living needs, such as mortgage/rent payments, utilities, food, gas, insurance, and childcare. These everyday essentials tend to be the easiest to identify, as they are frequently larger and recur at set intervals. Typically, these essentials make up 50 percent of your monthly spending. Essentials can be a little tricky, as it's easy for a need to fluctuate into a lifestyle expense. When you are reviewing your expenses, be honest with yourself. If something is not genuinely essential, label it appropriately. This is important because lifestyle expenses will likely be easier to reduce than everyday essentials.

For many women—particularly single moms like Elle—childcare costs comprise a significant amount of essential costs, impacting the balance of the framework. While childcare tends to default to everyday essentials, there are circumstances where the line between essentials and lifestyle blurs. Collins and James hired a nanny when she had her first child, Hayes. Two years later, they became a family of four with the addition of their daughter, Harper, and Collins decided to stay home with her children. With a newborn and toddler at home, they opted to keep the nanny while they adjusted to their new normal. Fast-forward, and four years later their nanny is still working part time.

As Collins fears the thought of life without a nanny, Elle pops into her mind. Elle never had a nanny; she's raising Ava as a single mother. This gives Collins pause—can she categorize her nanny as an essential expense? Collins decides to set this expense aside with a question mark until she gets through the rest of her expenses to determine where she should allocate it.

If you find that your essentials exceed 50 percent, review your expenses again and look for any essentials that could potentially be decreased and any that may be more appropriately labeled as lifestyle. Another example of lifestyle creeping into the essentials category is Jade's infatuation with fitness classes. For Jade fitness is an everyday essential, critical to her physical and mental health. She has a traditional gym membership at a large gym but also attends classes at studios all over town. Yoga, Pilates, spin, kickboxing: you name it, she does it, with each costing thirty dollars a class. When allocating her fitness spending, she realizes that her primary gym membership falls into the essentials category, but she isn't sure she can justify the additional studio visits as necessities.

GOALS AND RESERVES

After narrowing down your essentials, you want to prioritize your goals and reserves. Your reserves are your savings. This is the money you set aside for a rainy day, unexpected life expenses, and the goals that you outlined in chapter 1. Savings provide financial security and confidence—the foundation of building financial empowerment—

making this category a top priority in the framework.

Twenty percent of your income is a great target for building your reserves, but don't fret if you aren't quite there yet. Awareness is the key; start with the percentage you feel you can comfortably manage, and continue to work toward increasing the amount you are saving annually.

You do not have to earn a high income to set and meet goals for building your reserves. While Elle has the lowest annual income out of our trio of investors, she's highly motivated by her desire to stay out of debt while meeting her goals. This pushes her to make sure her reserves are where they need to be for her household. While it's not always easy to achieve as a single mom, doing so aligns with her values and priorities. Using this framework enables her to cover daily life and prioritize saving for the future while providing a little room for treating herself and Ava to fun today.

SAVINGS PROVIDE FINANCIAL SECURITY AND CONFIDENCE— THE FOUNDATION OF BUILDING FINANCIAL EMPOWERMENT.

EMERGENCY SAVINGS

Begin by making sure you have enough funds in your emergency savings. Emergency savings are earmarked for unexpected and often large expenses or life events. For most people an emergency savings fund should have reserves to cover essential living expenses for a minimum of six months (nine months if you are self-employed).

For some people, like Elle, having emergency savings that far exceed those guidelines may provide a greater sense of security. Start with the recommended minimum and determine what number makes you feel most confident. Your confidence number is the balance you should target and maintain. These funds should be held in a separate savings account and be used only to cover temporary loss of income, a medical emergency, emergency home expenses, or unexpected car repairs.

GOAL-BASED SAVINGS

The goals you set in chapter 1 should also be part of your savings plan. Depending on the time frame of your goal, there are various account types and investment options that can help you grow the funds, beyond a traditional savings account.

College Savings

Elle has been putting aside money for Ava's college fund since her birth. Between deposits and interest earned, the account has grown to $10,300 over the past eight years. Elle is doing a great job of saving for her daughter's education, but, as she told Jade during at the beginning of this chapter, she realizes that it will not be enough.

This exercise will help Elle determine whether she can afford to save more, but she will also consider investing the funds to earn more than interest from the bank. She makes a note to look into tax-advantaged ways she can invest for Ava's education, such as **529 college savings plans,**[5] **Coverdell education savings accounts (ESAs), and custodial accounts** including Uniform Gifts to Minors Act (UGMA) and Uniform Transfers to Minors Act (UTMA) accounts.

EMPOWER TIP: Start your college savings accounts early. Ask friends and family to make gifts to your child's college savings at birthdays and holidays. Those extra contributions can help boost your saving efforts.

Retirement Savings

There are multiple types of retirement savings vehicles. Let's take a closer look at the types of accounts that can be used and the important factors to consider when determining which retirement savings vehicles are right for you.[6]

When Elle first started working, one of her coworkers suggested she set up a **Roth Individual Retirement Account** (IRA) for her retirement savings. The woman told her that the monthly contributions Elle made would be with after-tax dollars, and the earnings would grow tax-free. Elle wasn't sure what all that meant, but her coworker was persistent with her advice, so Elle went to the bank and opened a Roth IRA.

As time went on and Elle learned more about her account, she realized how beneficial the advice turned out to be. While Elle does not receive tax deductions for the deposits she makes, her Roth IRA allows her earnings to accumulate tax-free. That means that her future withdrawals will be 100 percent tax-free, allowing her money to go further in retirement.

Elle's income continues to fall below the annual earnings limit, allowing her to contribute the maximum amount each year. By contributing the maximum amount and waiting until she is eligible to take withdrawals without a penalty (59.5 years old), Elle will benefit from thirty-five years of tax-free compounding growth.

EMPOWER TIP: The earlier you start saving, the more you will benefit from earning interest on your interest earnings, multiplying your money. That's the power of compounding!

In the future, if Elle's income exceeds the annual limits for a Roth

IRA, she would still be able to save for retirement using a **Traditional IRA.** The main difference between the two is when taxes are paid. The taxation of future distributions is an important consideration in how far retirement dollars will stretch.

Currently, with her Roth IRA, taxes are paid up front, when the dollars go in. With a Traditional IRA, earnings and deductible contributions grow tax deferred, meaning taxes are paid when money is withdrawn in retirement. Income limits and retirement plan options available through her employer will determine whether her contributions will be deemed pretax (deductible) or after tax (nondeductible). Since taxes have not been paid on all the dollars, there are mandated withdrawals from traditional IRAs starting at age seventy-two, and, as with a Roth, she would not be able to access the funds without penalty before age 59.5.

EMPOWER TIP: If you do not have earned income but your spouse does, you can and should contribute to an individual retirement account in your name.

With big dreams of retiring at age fifty-five, Jade has prioritized saving for retirement, participating in the 401(k) plan available through her work. **401(k)s, 403(b)s, thrift savings plans (TSPs), and profit-sharing plans** are all types of employer-sponsored retirement savings plans. Like most employer-sponsored plans, Jade's plan allows for both her and her employer to contribute to her account. Her plan outlines that her employer matches 100 percent of her contributions up to 3 percent of her compensation.

Jade's employer match is a great way to enhance her contributions. When she first started working, she contributed 3 percent of her salary to ensure she was receiving the maximum match. If she contributed less than that, she would have been leaving money on the table. As Jade received raises over time, she has increased her contribution to 10 percent. Employer-sponsored plans have no income limits and higher contribution limits than IRAs, which will allow her to continue increasing her contributions until she reaches the maximum annual contribution limit.

Just like IRAs, Jade's employer-sponsored plan allows her to elect whether she wants her employee contributions to be pretax (Traditional) or after-tax (Roth). Jade has elected to make pretax contributions, opting to pay the taxes in the future rather than today. The funds that Jade and her employer contribute go into a separate account in her name, where she is responsible for electing investment options and bears the investment risk. When Jade retires or changes jobs, her vested funds can remain in the plan, be transferred to a new employer's plan, or be rolled to an IRA.

> **EMPOWER TIP:** Give your future self a raise every time you receive an increase in pay. Increase your employee contributions by 20 percent (or more) of your pay increase until you reach the maximum annual contribution limit.

Health Savings

Jade also makes contributions to a **Health Savings Account (HSA)**, which can be used for qualified healthcare expenses. Jade is eligible to make contributions to an HSA since she participates in a high-deductible healthcare plan. A major benefit of an HSA is that Jade can use the funds to cover insurance deductibles, doctor visits, and other healthcare costs now and in retirement.

If you are eligible for an HSA, contributions can be made by you or your employer up to the annual maximum. Possibly the biggest benefit of an HSA is the triple tax benefit: contributions are pretax (tax deductible), earnings grow tax-free, and qualified withdrawals are tax-free. Like employer-sponsored retirement plans, HSAs are portable and can move with you if you change jobs.

> **EMPOWER TIP:** If you are eligible for an HSA, target a *minimum* account balance equal to your annual deductible. When a major unexpected medical issue arises, you will have the funds on hand to meet your deductible.

Whether you are saving for a rainy day, your child's education, or your own retirement, there may be an account type that allows you to make your savings more advantageous, and there are certainly more investment vehicles than what I have listed here. Deferred compensation, flexible savings accounts (FSAs), and employee stock purchase plans, for example, may be relevant to you too.

But most importantly, target a 20 percent savings rate across all categories. If you are already putting 8 percent into your 401(k), that leaves 12 percent to allocate to the rest of your goals. Keep in mind that 20 percent is a guideline. Create a system that works for you and supports your long-term goals. For instance, if you want to maintain a higher level of emergency funds, like Elle, or retire early, like Jade, you may need to save more than 20 percent. This may mean that you have less to spend in the lifestyle category, but living debt-free and retiring early *are* lifestyle choices.

LIFESTYLE

The last spending category is lifestyle. The simplest way to think about this category of spending is as a *need* versus a *want*. It's the money that you spend on a nice dinner, a vacation, or retail therapy—it's your lifestyle. Lifestyle money is the first place to cut back when you want to increase your savings. When added up, the seemingly small discretionary expenses can ultimately take a huge chunk out of your budget. How many times a week do you buy a coffee on your way to work? How frequently do you eat out each month? How many subscription services do you pay for? What do expenses like these cost you weekly, monthly, annually? If you want to curb spending and bulk up reserves, lifestyle is the place to look.

> REMEMBER, IT CAN BE EASY TO UNINTENTIONALLY CATEGORIZE LIFESTYLE CHOICES AS ESSENTIAL EXPENSES.

Remember, it can be easy to unintentionally categorize lifestyle choices as essential expenses. When considering your essential versus lifestyle expenses, be honest with yourself about how an expense should be categorized. Let's take a closer look at the distinction between the two with our investors.

Having a car, for example, can be essential—you need it to get to work—but at what point does a car become a lifestyle expense? For years Jade drove a Prius and had no car payment. The car was well maintained and fully paid for. But recently, she decided to upgrade her Prius to a Lexus and take on a $450 monthly payment. Jade must ask herself, *Is that essential?* Is it truly a necessity to own a luxury car, or should the difference in cost be allocated to lifestyle choice?

Childcare is another expense that falls in this gray area. Collins put a question mark next to childcare when she started looking at her spending. She now finds that she should categorize this expense under lifestyle. Having a nanny was essential when she was working. But now that she is at home, it has become a lifestyle choice. In fact, as the kids get older, she starts to wonder whether they could further reduce this expense by supplementing their childcare needs with an occasional babysitter.

When looking at expenses in the lifestyle category, you are ultimately trying to determine whether you are living within your means. We all want nice things but should avoid splurging on them at the expense of needs or savings. This can be challenging, as it requires being brutally honest with ourselves. And when we become accustomed to certain lifestyle treats—going to the nail salon when you have polish at home, daily coffeehouse visits, ordering takeout versus cooking, etc.—it's easy to justify them and hard to let them go. But remember that saving today is an investment in your future self.

HOW DID OUR INVESTORS FARE?[7]

Elle's spending and saving profile is 60/20/20. To reach her $1,000-a-month savings target, Elle puts $300 into her emergency savings account, $500 into her Roth IRA, $100 into savings for Ava's education, and $100 into her vacation fund. While she does not have a set monthly goal for her down payment, she has been saving her bonuses in a goal-based account and targets $5,000 per year. Childcare costs for Ava result in her spending more on her everyday essential needs, leaving less to allocate to lifestyle expenses. While she has less to allocate to lifestyle, Elle feels this exercise affirms she is on the right path with her savings.

ELLE	After-tax monthly income: $5,000	Profile: 60/20/20
Account	**Current Balance**	**Monthly Savings**
Emergency savings	$50,000	$300
Roth IRA	$104,000	$500
Ava's education	$10,300	$100
Down payment	$30,000	Annual bonus
Travel fund	$2,000	$100

Jade's spending and savings break down to 50/20/30, saving $2,000 per month. Being goal oriented, she has allocated monthly savings to each of her goals. For her retirement goals, she puts a total of $1,000 per month into her 401(k) and $300 into her HSA. She has been allocating the balance of her monthly savings to emergency savings but decided to create a new savings account for her investment property. Going forward, she plans to contribute $350 to her down payment fund and $350 to emergency savings.

JADE	After-tax monthly income: $10,000	Profile: 50/20/30
Account	Current Balance	Monthly Savings
Emergency savings	$50,000	$350
401(k)	$150,000	$1,000
HSA	$11,250	$300
Investment property	$0	$350

Collins estimates that her household spending and savings ratio is off balance, at 50/10/40. Truthfully, she is not quite sure what her household expenses are or how much she and her husband, James, are saving. She plans to work with James to clarify these categories for their household. Anticipating that their spending is in excess of their target range, she commits to decreasing her lifestyle spending by 10 percent over the next six months. She is excited to share her goal of monitoring and mindful spending with James and work together to understand their current circumstances together.

COLLINS	After-tax monthly income: $25,000	Profile: 50/10/40
Account	Current Balance	Monthly Savings
Emergency savings	$30,000	No set amount
401(k) (James)	$275,000	$1,250
Stock account	$500,000	No set amount

EMPOWER TIP: If you're married or have a partner, work on these goals together so you are both committed to your shared goals and can keep each other accountable.

Now is the time to see how you fare. Start by reviewing the last two to six months of pay stubs and bank and credit card statements so you can see *where* your money is going. The goal is to categorize the expenses into those three main categories. Chances are you will be surprised by what you find.

It can be difficult to take a candid look at where you are spending your money. It is important to note that this exercise is intended to create awareness. The more you know about your spending, the more empowered you will feel to make proactive changes. The goal here is not perfection. It is to look at your spending and make subtle tweaks over time, becoming more mindful in your spending and intentional with your saving.

WHAT IF YOU COME OUT ON TOP?

You have looked at all your expenses, and you fall in line with the 50/20/30 rule, or your own target ratio profile, if you are looking to save more. Congratulations! The next step is to dig a little deeper and make sure that this ratio still supports the goals you outlined in chapter 1.

Let's check in with Elle and Jade to see if they are on track for their goals:

ELLE'S MIDTERM GOALS	Ava's education	New house
Separate savings account?	Yes	Yes
Timeline	10 years	5 years
Target amount	$40,000	$70,000
Current amount	$10,300	$30,000
Annual savings target	$1,200	$3,000
On track?	No	No

JADE'S MID- AND LONG-TERM GOALS	Investment property	Retirement
Separate savings account	No	Yes
Timeline	5 years	17 years
Target amount	$30,000	$1,000,000
Current amount	$0	$105,000
Annual savings target	$350	$12,000
On track?	No	No

It's always important to look at the full picture. While Elle and Jade are on target for the percentage of their income they are saving, they have uncovered that their goals will not be achieved in their desired timelines. In part II, we will see how they increase their contributions to these savings goals when the opportunities arise and, when appropriate, use investments to increase the probability of achieving their goals in their desired time frames.

> **EMPOWER TIP:** If you are not on track to achieving your goals, you can reassess your target savings, revise your timeline, or identify other steps to make your goals more achievable.

If you are on track with your goals, revisit them and see whether you want to make any changes or whether you have new goals to add. You also want to have a plan for when you have positive income changes in the future. You may get a raise at work or finally pay off those pesky student loans. More money is always exciting, but now what do you do with it? Avoid the temptation to expand into your new wealth and spend it elsewhere. Extra money can get spent quickly on your lifestyle. Be sure that you are intentional about your savings.

ASK YOURSELF WHETHER THERE ARE ANY SPENDING OR SAVING HABITS YOU WANT TO CHANGE. THERE IS ALWAYS ROOM FOR IMPROVEMENT!

Finally, ask yourself whether there are any spending or saving habits you want to change. There is always room for improvement!

WHAT IF YOUR SAVINGS FALL SHORT?

If after completing this exercise you find that you aren't saving enough for your current situation, don't panic. There are some simple things you can do to reevaluate and make progress toward your target spending and saving ratio.

Changing spending habits and building savings takes time. Be patient and prepare to make your way to your goals gradually. It is also important to be realistic when you are looking at your expenses. If you are used to going out to social events often, a severe cutback may not be reasonable. Perhaps start by limiting your nights out to once a week instead of three times a week, or committing to saving $100 a month and seeing how that affects your social spending.

Consider an online tracking tool if you are like Collins and do not have the time or interest to manually track your spending. Many banks and financial institutions offer these tools. You can also use third-party sites that allow you to monitor your spending on demand. By showing you what you are spending in real time, these tools can help you stay within the savings parameters you set for yourself. Conversely, the tools can also create positive reinforcement, as they will track your progress to your goals.

> CHANGING SPENDING HABITS AND BUILDING SAVINGS TAKES TIME. BE PATIENT AND PREPARE TO MAKE YOUR WAY TO YOUR GOALS GRADUALLY.

These tools and the 50/20/30 rule are ways for you to *budget*. Even though women value financial security, we do not necessarily like the B-word. The majority of us dislike budgeting because we associate it with living a restricted existence, but budgeting can be empowering.

The goals you set are great ways to get inspired, narrow your focus, and stay motivated to save money.

This exercise has motivated Collins to be more mindful with her spending and re-enforced the need to set SMART goals. She plans to track her lifestyle spending and pinpoint a few items that rack up high bills. While she is committed to spending 10 percent less, she should also set savings metrics for each of her goals and track her progress. Tracking your progress is important to reinforce beneficial behavior and give you an opportunity to celebrate when you are successful. It is imperative to acknowledge the little wins and treat yourself. If we forget to reward ourselves, budgeting can feel punitive in the short term. Being intentional with our spending and saving is crucial to ensuring that we have strong financial futures.

COLLINS'S SHORT-TERM GOALS	New car	Dream vacation
Separate savings account?	No	No
Timeline	2 years	1 year
Target amount	$40,000	$15,000
Current amount	$0	$0
Annual savings target	$0	$0
On track?	No	No

TAKE ACTION!

Determining your personal 50/20/30 ratio profile is powerful for identifying areas where you may be spending too much or saving too little. I know that looking at your income and then breaking down your expenses can be humbling, but it can also be extremely empowering. Even if you don't like what you have uncovered, now you know where your money goes, and *knowledge is power.*

Using the goals that you created in chapter 1 as inspiration, **ENVISION** how you can be more intentional with your spending and savings to help you achieve your financial goals:

E   **EMPOWER** yourself by allowing space to make improvements over time.

N   **NARROW** your focus by tracking your spending, and set savings goals that support your larger goals.

V   **VALIDATE** that your goals are realistic and fall within your 50/20/30 framework.

I   **IMPLEMENT** your plan by increasing your savings today, even if it is only a small amount.

S   **SHARE** your goals with others by letting your loved ones know you are committed to making these changes.

I   **INCENTIVIZE** yourself by establishing milestones for your goals, and celebrate when you reach them.

O   **OVERSEE** your progress every six months to make sure you are on track.

N   **NAVIGATE** life events, both good and bad, that may cause you to modify your spending and saving plan.

CHAPTER THREE

BORROWING BASICS

September

"I've got it," Collins says, offering to pick up the bill after our investors have reached the end of one of their lunch dates. As Collins reaches for her card, she accidentally drops her wallet. A handful of credit cards clatter to the floor.

"Wow," exclaims Elle as she bends over to pick them up. "How many credit cards do you have?"

Collins shrugs. "Most of them give me early access to great sales or points that our family uses to travel."

But as Collins puts the cards back into her wallet, she feels uneasy thinking about the goals she made to start budgeting and rein in her lifestyle spending. Suddenly a rainbow of credit cards doesn't feel so good.

"I should do something about this," Collins admits.

"What?" asks Elle.

"All these cards. I don't need to have so many, and I don't really know what the balance is on any of them. They certainly can't be moving me toward my goals."

Elle nods. "You know, I'm worried about carrying debt. That's why I've never had a credit card."

"Oh, I'm not in debt," Collins whispers under her breath, so quietly that Elle doesn't hear.

Debt can be a confusing term because it tends to have negative connotations, but not all debt is bad. It is often unrealistic to achieve some of your larger goals without financing a portion of them. Homeownership, automobiles, and small businesses typically involve borrowing money to help make these goals a reality. However, using debt to live beyond your means can become difficult to pay for and take money away from the goals you are striving to achieve.

BEFORE YOU BORROW

Perhaps you are like Elle: you're scared of credit cards because of the potential to rack up debt. Or maybe you are more like Collins: you have many credit cards and have just received an invitation to apply for yet another one. Before you pull the trigger on your next borrowing decision, it is important to understand the mechanics of any debt you currently have and how additional borrowing will impact your journey to financial empowerment. Making sound financial decisions around debt is critical to financial stability today and in the future. Before we identify the different types of debt you can use to achieve your goals and those that can derail them, let's explore the steps you should take to be in a good position to borrow money.

UNDERSTAND YOUR CREDIT SCORE

Your credit score reflects how well you have managed your credit and therefore how creditworthy you are. This three-digit score typically ranges from 300 to 850. The higher your score, the greater confidence lenders have making loans to you, allowing you to qualify for better terms. There are different types of scores; here is a look at the range of FICO credit scores and how they are calculated.

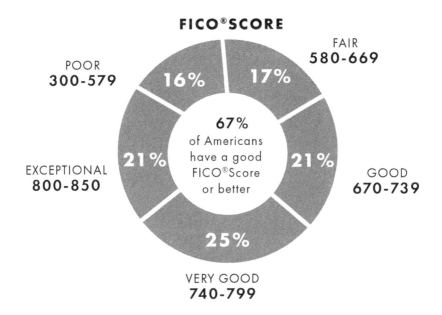

FICO®SCORE

FAIR
580-669

POOR
300-579

16%

17%

67%
of Americans
have a good
FICO®Score
or better

21%

21%

EXCEPTIONAL
800-850

GOOD
670-739

25%

VERY GOOD
740-799

Source: "What Is a Good Credit Score?," Experian.com, https:// www.experian.com/blogs/ask-experian/credit-education/score-basics/ what-is-a-good-credit-score/.

EMPOWER TIP: Target a FICO Score of 740 or higher to receive better-than-average borrowing rates.

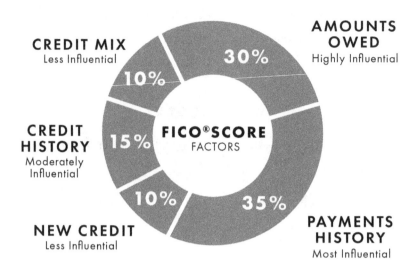

CREDIT MIX
Less Influential

AMOUNTS OWED
Highly Influential

CREDIT HISTORY
Moderately Influential

NEW CREDIT
Less Influential

PAYMENTS HISTORY
Most Influential

FICO®SCORE FACTORS

10%
30%
15%
10%
35%

Source: "What Is a Good Credit Score?," Experian.com, https://
www.experian.com/blogs/ask-experian/credit-education/score-basics/
what-is-a-good-credit-score/.

Your credit score is an important piece of your financial empowerment and should be monitored annually. Most banks or credit card companies allow you to access your credit score each year, or you can request a free copy of your credit report from the three main credit bureaus at AnnualCreditReport.com. In addition to monitoring your score, check your credit report to make sure the information is accurate. Know what your credit score is, and if it's not quite where it should be, set goals to help you to get there.

With your payment history on credit cards and loans impacting your credit score the most, it is essential to prioritize making on-time payments. Missed payments and even late payments (over thirty days) will remain on your credit report for seven years, making payment history a challenging place to make up ground improving your credit score.

EMPOWER TIP: Automatic payments can help you avoid an accidental late or missed payment, helping to maintain a strong credit score.

Fortunately, making small changes in other categories can improve your credit score in a matter of months. The total amount of outstanding debt you owe is the next most impactful metric. Your credit utilization rate measures the amount you owe relative to the amount you have available—in other words, how close you are to reaching your credit limits. To determine your credit utilization rate, simply divide your total outstanding balance by your total credit limit. The lower your utilization rate, the better; 30 percent or less is ideal.

In checking her credit score, Collins finds that she has a lower than expected credit score of 674 due to a handful of late payments and high utilization rate. Collins's available credit across all cards is $50,000. She is currently utilizing $32,500, or about 65 percent of her available credit. With goals to decrease spending, Collins anticipates she will be able to pay down her credit card balances more rapidly. With credit reporting agencies updating monthly, it could take only two to three credit cycles before changes are reflected in her credit score.

EMPOWER TIP: To strengthen your credit score, target paying your full statement balance on your credit cards each month and keep your credit utilization rate below 30 percent.

While Collins wants to work to decrease the number of credit cards she has, she should be mindful about closing credit card accounts. Closing an account will reduce her total revolving available credit, which could result in her further increasing her utilization rate, the opposite of what she is trying to accomplish. Once Collins pays down her outstanding balances and limits her use to one or two primary credit cards, she can inquire about increasing her credit limits on those cards.

She'll want to confirm that they increase her limit using a soft credit inquiry. When you check your own credit score or a lender checks your credit as part of a preapproval process, it's considered a soft credit inquiry, which does not affect your credit score. A hard credit inquiry occurs when a lender checks your credit history as part of the approval process, which will impact your credit score.

When checking her credit score, Elle finds that her lack of debt use has resulted in her not having enough credit history for a strong credit score. Having always been nervous about borrowing money, she has no debt, which means creditors do not have enough information to know how trustworthy a borrower she is. She did not realize that her lack of credit history, and therefore her low credit score of 580, could potentially be a roadblock when the time comes for her to buy a house.

Elle discovers that credit card use is the quickest way to build good credit and decides to open a secured credit card to create credit and payment history. This type of credit card is backed by a cash deposit, reducing the risk to the issuer of the credit card. Elle plans to use the card for everyday essential purchases, such as gas or groceries, and will start to see her score increase over the course of the year.

CALCULATE YOUR DEBT-TO-INCOME RATIO

When considering taking out a loan, it's important to be confident that you can afford the loan payments. The spending and saving exercise in chapter 2 will help you uncover how much capacity you have for additional debt payments that are categorized as essential expenses. You should also calculate your debt-to-income (DTI) ratio.

Your DTI ratio compares how much you owe each month to how much you earn each month. Specifically, it's the percentage of your monthly income (before taxes) that goes toward payments for auto loans, credit cards, student loans, mortgages, and other debts. Lenders use this number to help determine your ability to afford the additional debt payments for which you are applying. The more debt you have, the higher your DTI ratio.

EMPOWER TIP: A DTI ratio between 20 and 30 percent will enable you to comfortably cover the rest of your everyday essential expenses without exceeding the 50-percent-of-income target.

With a credit score of 785, Jade is in a good credit position to borrow. But since she already has a mortgage, student loan, and car loan, she wonders what monthly payment amount she could afford when purchasing another investment property.

Jade's *before-tax* monthly income is $12,000. To keep her DTI ratio at a conservative 25 percent, the maximum total debt payments she would want to have are $3,000. Her current monthly debt payments include a $1,450 mortgage payment on a rental home, a $450 auto loan payment, a $275 student loan payment, and a $50 minimum credit card payment. Totaling these expenses

WHEN CONSIDERING TAKING OUT A LOAN, IT'S IMPORTANT TO BE CONFIDENT THAT YOU CAN AFFORD THE LOAN PAYMENTS.

brings her current monthly debt payments to $2,225, leaving her only $775 per month to meet future debt-payment obligations. This is an important exercise for Jade. She discovers that she is limited in how much new mortgage debt she wants to take on, even as an expense shared with Logan.

After requesting current credit scores, reviewing their credit reports for any discrepancies, and calculating their DTI, our investors have identified areas they want to improve to make themselves more attractive borrowers. Being in a strong position to qualify for the best borrowing terms will help in achieving larger goals that may require bank financing.

ELLE

Credit score of 580

Debt-to-income ratio of less than 10 percent

Elle's low credit score is the biggest deterrent in qualifying for a loan. Having and using her credit card will help raise her credit score and build her confidence managing debt. Both will be important when she looks to borrow more substantial amounts in the future.

COLLINS

Credit score of 674 (James's is 690)

Debt-to-income ratio of 35 percent

Collins's and James's credit scores and debt-to-income ratios will be major factors when lenders consider the terms of any borrowing they look to do. They will want to increase their credit scores and decrease their DTI to qualify for more favorable loan terms.

JADE

Credit score of 785

Debt-to-income ratio of 18.75 percent

Jade's high credit score will be beneficial in qualifying for favorable terms, but she will want to consider her DTI before taking on more debt. Since her plan includes making an "ours" real estate investment with Logan, his credit score and debt-to-income ratio will be important pieces of their borrowing picture. Beyond understanding these key credit factors, Jade also wants to assess their individual net worths.

NET WORTH

Your net worth is the difference in the value of the items you **own** (assets) minus outstanding debt balances you **owe** (liabilities). When you outline your goals and work to increase your savings, build assets, decrease spending, and reduce debt, you are actually working to increase your net worth. Knowing your net worth will help you understand your current financial situation and provide an overall benchmark for your financial empowerment.

Calculating your net worth is relatively straightforward. Pull together a list of the assets that you own (e.g., bank accounts, investment accounts, real estate, automobiles, art, jewelry, and other high-value items) and conservatively estimate their current value. From this total, subtract your total liabilities (e.g., your credit card and loan balances). This is your **net worth**. It may be positive or negative, large or small. Do not get discouraged if this number is not currently where you want it to be. The nature of this calculation is such that it should grow over time. When considering borrowing, it is important to think about how it will impact your net worth.

ESSENTIAL VERSUS LIFESTYLE DEBT

Debt is often categorized as "good" debt or "bad" debt. The concept of "good" debt is about borrowing funds that will allow you to invest in valuable assets that grow or generate income in the future, such as mortgages, student loans, and business loans. "Bad" debt involves borrowing money to purchase depreciating assets or make unnecessary purchases, such as certain auto loans, credit cards, and other consumer debts.

But life is not always so black and white. Rather than categorize debt as good versus bad, I like to categorize debt by which spending category it falls into: essential versus lifestyle.

ESSENTIAL DEBT

Essential debt can help build ownership, grow your income, and enhance your net worth over time. In addition to investing in appreciating assets, low-interest debt can allow you to leverage your income to obtain higher-cost essential items.

MORTGAGES

If you are a homeowner or aspire to be one, then a mortgage is likely part of your financial plan. With the high cost of real estate, mortgages or home loans can help make homeownership an achievable goal. When you have a mortgage, you make payments to the lender, slowly decreasing the amount of your loan (liability) and increasing the equity in your house (asset). Thus, owning a home can help you build your net worth gradually.

Taking out a loan to purchase a home can be one of the biggest financial decisions you make in your lifetime. Before you start looking for houses, you should engage an experienced real estate agent and qualified loan officer to walk you through the home buying and financing process from start to finish. You will want to determine your preferred monthly payment and factor in out-of-pocket expenses like your down payment and closing costs. Knowing these key pieces will provide a starting point for you and your mortgage broker to explore what type of mortgage is right for you and allow you to get preapproved for a loan.

There are two main types of mortgages: government-backed mortgages and private mortgages. Federal Housing Administration (FHA) loans are a type of **government-backed mortgage** commonly used by first-time home buyers. The fact that these loans are backed by the government enables borrowers to have lower minimum down payments and lower credit scores than for other mortgages, though there are a number of stipulations, including an additional expense of FHA mortgage insurance.

A **private mortgage** is any home loan that is not backed by a government entity. The Federal National Mortgage Association (Fannie Mae) and the Federal Home Loan Mortgage Corporation (Freddie Mac) set the guidelines for these loans. With no government insurance on these loans, lenders will further assess a borrower's financial health to reduce the risk of lending. Lenders also look for other ways to mitigate risk, such as private mortgage insurance (PMI), when borrowers seek more than 80 percent of the property value.

Beyond considering what percentage of the property value you plan to borrow, it is also important to understand whether the total planned loan amount is within conventional borrowing limits. **Jumbo loans** are also called nonconforming loans because they exceed the limits set by the Federal Housing Finance Agency. The high loan amount of jumbo loans creates an additional layer of risk, resulting in higher mortgage rates being applied to compensate the lender.

EMPOWER TIP: While you might be willing to pay higher rates for a mortgage that exceeds conforming borrowing limits, avoid higher rates due to lower credit and down payments by looking to government-backed loans.

It is important to educate yourself about your options and consider not just the monthly payment but the total loan costs and full interest amount you will pay over the lifetime of the loan. For any mortgage being in a strong overall borrowing position will enable you to receive the most favorable loan terms, resulting in substantial savings over the lifetime of your loan.

Managing Mortgage Debt

If your credit has improved, interest rates have changed, or your loan-to-value ratio has decreased, you may be able to refinance your mortgage with more favorable terms. Lower interest rates create the greatest opportunity to save money over the lifetime of your loan. If current rates have fallen 1 percent or more below your current interest rate, it may be beneficial for you to refinance. Refinancing typically costs 2 to 6 percent of your remaining loan amount. Before you refinance, determine how long it will take for your monthly savings to recoup these costs by calculating your break-even point.

Collins notes that she and James should investigate refinancing their mortgage. When they purchased their home, the value of their mortgage exceeded conventional borrowing limits, making it a jumbo loan. Their current mortgage balance of $625,000 is below jumbo limits, which would allow them to borrow at a lower rate. If they wait until they increase their household credit score, they will be in an even better position to qualify for the best rates available.

But remember, there are always costs to getting a loan. Collins estimates that the cost to refinance would be around $15,000. If refinancing decreases their mortgage payment by $500 per month, it would take two and a half years to recoup the cost. Because they plan to stay in the house at least until the kids go to college, the long-term savings outweigh the up-front cost, and saving $500 a month over the life of their loan would be substantial savings!

EMPOWER TIP: After refinancing, consider making additional principal payments with the savings. You will pay off your mortgage faster and reduce the amount of interest you pay over the life of your loan.

Other opportunities to reduce the total interest you will pay include locking in a fixed rate if you have an adjustable-rate mortgage, decreasing your loan period, or removing insurance expenses. If you are carrying additional mortgage expenses, such as PMI or FHA mortgage insurance, know when you can request to have them removed or refinance if advantageous. Always analyze the costs to confirm that refinancing will put you in a better financial position overall.

STUDENT LOANS

A student loan can be a critical resource in setting yourself up for future financial empowerment—an investment in your education will last a lifetime. Similar to mortgages, student loans typically fall into two categories: federal and private.

Federal student loan programs are created and funded by the US Department of Education. Federal student loan options are the best place to start if you or a family member needs help covering college education expenses. Federal loans are just one component of a financial aid package; your school may also award scholarships, grants, and work-study opportunities. Once you have a clear picture of the entire aid package, you can determine whether you also want to apply for private student loans. **Private student loans** are made by private institutions, such as banks, and are structured similarly to mortgages and other bank loans.

Federal and private student loans make funds for education easily accessible, but it is important to make good borrowing choices, as a student loan is a mid- to long-term debt. Key factors such as credit score, interest rates, repayment, and loan forgiveness are important aspects to consider when exploring student loan options.

Managing Student Loan Debt

With more than $1.6 trillion in outstanding student loan debt, student loans are the second-highest consumer debt category, after mortgages.[8] The high cost of higher education results in more than 50 percent of students needing to borrow funds to cover their education costs.[9] While it can feel like a heavy burden to come out of school saddled with debt, it's important to not feel strangled by it. The key is to make a plan that accounts for these payments in a manageable way.

Jade graduated with multiple federal student loans. For the first few years after school, she was paying each of them separately before she learned that she could combine them into a single direct consolidated loan. When she consolidated her $35,000 in loans, she was able to have a single monthly payment of $275 and a fixed interest rate of 5 percent (based on the weighted average of the interest rates of the original loans) and to select a payoff period of fifteen years (you can elect up to thirty years). Consolidating her loans enabled Jade to create a repayment plan that allows her to pay off the loan on her own terms.

There can be downsides to consolidation. For instance, having a longer loan period means that you could end up paying more in interest over the lifetime of the loan. Additionally, if you are eligible for loan forgiveness or an income-driven repayment plan, you'll want to understand the impact consolidating would have on those benefits.

Private student loans cannot be consolidated in the same way federal student loans can. To combine private student loans, you would need to refinance them. Refinancing private student loans can make sense if you want to save on interest or change your repayment terms. As with mortgage refi-

EDUCATE YOURSELF ON ALL YOUR OPTIONS, AND MAKE SURE THERE ARE LONG-TERM FINANCIAL BENEFITS TO REFINANCING.

nancing, educate yourself on all your options, and make sure there are long-term financial benefits to refinancing.

AUTO LOANS

Buying a new car is another major purchase that most people finance. As we saw in Jade's 50/20/30 exercise, car payments can easily shift from essentials to lifestyle. The key to avoiding lifestyle car debt is to plan ahead and be prepared. Before you start shopping for a new car, start with how much car you can afford and whether you want to purchase new versus previously owned.

Cars are depreciating assets, losing 20 percent of their value by the end of the first year and approximately 15 percent a year after that. That means that after five years, a new car loses 60 percent of its value.[10] Buying a previously owned vehicle can help you avoid the steep up-front depreciation costs, enabling your car to hold its resale value better.

If you are financing your purchase, the majority of the expense will be in your monthly car payment. These payments will most likely fall into your essentials category of spending. Be sure to consider your down payment and additional purchase costs, as well as your loan period and any prepayment penalties. There are also ongoing costs of vehicle ownership, such as insurance, registration fees, and maintenance. If you are spending more than fits in your essentials framework, it will spill over to your lifestyle category.

> **EMPOWER TIP:** Be cautious of lower payment amounts that are created by longer loan periods. You will pay less each month but more over time. It's best to have a shorter-term loan on a depreciating asset.

Auto loans are available through dealerships, banks, and credit unions. Before going to dealerships to start car shopping, contact your bank and local credit unions to get a loan quote. Know the terms they offer, and get preapproved for a loan. Just as with any other loan, your creditworthiness is an important factor in the terms for which you are able to qualify. Knowing the terms you can get at your bank or credit union will put you in a position of strength when you go to the dealership, where they will most likely want to discuss dealer financing.

> **EMPOWER TIP:** It's best to comparison shop for loans over a short period of time. Credit reporting agencies group multiple lender inquiries that occur within a fourteen-day period as a single inquiry, resulting in minimal impact to your credit score.

If you plan to trade in your vehicle, know the current resale value. The dealership wants to buy it at a lower cost than they can sell it for, enabling them to make a profit. Trading in your vehicle may be less of a hassle than selling it yourself, but make sure you are not leaving money on the table. The more money you receive for your trade-in value, the lower the amount you need to borrow.

Whether it is purchase price, loan terms, or trade-in value, it is important to get the best deal you can on an asset that will depreciate in value.

BUSINESS LOANS

If you own a small business or have a goal of starting one, at some point you will likely need or want to borrow money. A business loan can be a great source of capital, but knowing which loan is best for you and your business can be challenging.

There are many loan options available to help you invest and grow your small business. Conventional bank loans, online working capital loans, and peer-to-peer loans are just a few. Establish a relationship with a lender, and work together to determine which type of loan would make the most sense for your business.

Lenders will look at your credit, income and cash flow, business track record, current debt level, and assets that can be used as collateral, as well as the risk type of your business. These factors will determine the type and terms of your loan. Just as you would with a personal loan, you want to demonstrate that your business is a worthy borrower. The best way to do that is to have a legitimate business plan and all your financial documents in order, showing that your business is in a strong financial position.

As with any loan, have a plan for not only how you will use the money from the loan but how you will pay it back. Proper preparation and sound financial decisions can give you the best chance for qualifying for and repaying your business loan.

> **EMPOWER TIP:** Many small business loans require personal guarantees. Be mindful of the amounts that you are borrowing and what you are comfortable carrying as a liability.

LIFESTYLE DEBT

Lifestyle debt is when you use debt to inflate your lifestyle—that is, spending money you do not have on lavish dinners, designer clothes, and extravagant vacations. Lifestyle debt can become "bad" debt because it can be difficult to pay off, taking money away from the goals you are striving to achieve. Remember, your goals and financial decisions are blocks that build on each other. Making smart financial decisions around debt is critical to financial stability in the future.

Credit Cards

Credit cards can be the biggest culprit in lifestyle debt. Credit card debt is also called **revolving credit**, as it is intended to be paid off every month. Think of your credit card as a substitute for cash, not a way to borrow money. Proper use of credit cards can be financially beneficial. They help you build and maintain good credit, provide a layer of security and protection, enable you to earn rewards and cash-back incentives, and allow you to manage your cash flow.

Choose a credit card that matches your spending habits. Are you looking for a basic credit card, or are you interested in earning points or rewards? How do you intend to use the card? Is the credit limit high enough? Will the card be widely accepted at different businesses and in other countries? What perks and security features does the card offer? Be aware of your credit card spending and diligent about your payments, maximizing your credit card benefits with little cost to you. If you use your credit card wisely and pay it off monthly, you can use many credit cards for free (unless you pay an annual fee).

Know Your Interest Rate and Fees

There is always a cost to borrowing money. Make sure that you understand what those costs are and comparison shop. If you carry a credit card balance, it's important that you understand the interest charges and what other fees you might be paying. These **terms and conditions** are outlined in your cardholder agreement. The cardholder agreement is a legally binding contract between you and the credit issuer that outlines the following:

- your credit limit;

- your annual percentage rate (APR) for purchases, balance transfers, and cash advances (different APRs may be applied to each);

- how your APR is calculated;

- how your minimum payment is calculated;

- fees that can be charged for late payments, overlimit charges, returned payments, etc., as well as annual fees; and

- how disputes will be resolved.

EMPOWER TIP: Your credit card issuer can and will change the terms of your agreement over time. Make sure to read any notifications regarding changes to your cardholder agreement.

Let's explore how the cost of interest can add to an overall expense. Collins and James recently went on a seven-day vacation to Hawaii. Their vacation costs included $1,350 in airfare and $750 a day for their hotel, dining, and entertainment. The total cost of their vacation was $6,600. If they had identified their vacation as a short-term goal, they could have saved $550 per month for twelve months and covered the cost of the trip. Instead, they charged the entire vacation to their travel-points credit card with a plan to pay it over time.

Paying the same $550 per month they could have saved, it will take them fourteen months to pay off their credit card, and they will pay over $700 in interest. Applying this same principle to multiple purchases, Collins finds that she is paying thousands of dollars in interest that could be going toward her savings goals.

Managing Lifestyle Debt

Striving to become free of lifestyle debt will enable you to make your money work *for* you. Rather than paying high interest rates to lenders, you can earn interest on the money you save. The secret to managing lifestyle debt is to not buy things you can't afford. Instead, set a goal and save until you have enough money to pay for the purchase.

Having emergency funds and savings targets for your goals will also help prevent you from building up lifestyle debt. After going through the spending and saving exercise in chapter 2, you should be aware of any spending habits that you need to change. If you, like Collins, find yourself with lifestyle debt, create a plan to pay it off.

Collins starts by making a list of the amounts that she owes. With a goal to pay $1,500 per month, she determines it will take her just over two years to pay off the debt. She will continue to make her minimum payments on each card and make additional payments to the card with the smallest amount owed first and, when that card is fully paid off, make additional payments on the next-smallest balance. This process will eliminate card balances quickly, snowballing as she gets closer to having only one monthly credit card payment. Once she has paid off all her outstanding balances, she plans to pay the full balance each month.

When managing your credit cards:

- Know your interest rate and fees.
- If you already have good credit, request a lower interest rate.
- Use less than 30 percent of your total available credit limit.
- Minimize the number of cards you have.
- Review your statements for inaccurate or fraudulent charges.
- Pay more than the minimum, ideally the full balance, every month.
- Sign up for autopay to ensure on-time payments.

TAKE ACTION!

An easy way to think about how to use debt properly is to ask yourself, "How will this benefit my future self?" Being conscious and purposeful with the debt you choose to take on will help you make the best decisions, not just for today but for the long term. Properly using debt can allow you to increase your net worth and responsibly achieve the goals that you have set for yourself.

As our investors have, identify steps that you can take today to ensure you are in the best borrowing position, and consider how debt fits into your long-term financial picture. **ENVISION** the position you want to be in as you work to achieve financial empowerment.

E   **EMPOWER** yourself by knowing your credit score. Target a FICO Score of 740 or higher.

N   **NARROW** your focus to borrowing that supports your long-term goals and increases your net worth.

V   **VALIDATE** your ability to use financing to achieve your goals. Target a debt-to-income ratio that fits within your 50/20/30 profile.

I   **IMPLEMENT** your plan utilizing the most favorable borrowing terms available to you.

S   **SHARE** your progress in paying down lifestyle debt. Keep your credit utilization rate below 30 percent.

I   **INCENTIVIZE** yourself, celebrating when you eliminate debt obligations and improve your credit score.

O   **OVERSEE** your debt liabilities, and monitor your credit score annually.

N   **NAVIGATE** life along the way by remaining a creditworthy borrower; you never know when you might want a loan.

CHAPTER FOUR

PROTECT YOURSELF

October

"Did you hear about Kristin?" asks Collins, pulling up a stool at Jade's kitchen island.

"No," says Jade as she cuts vegetables to go with her freshly made hummus. "I've lost track of her over the years."

Taking a deep breath, Collins says, "She passed away on Thursday."

"What happened?" gasps Elle.

"She had a really aggressive form of breast cancer. It was so far advanced, it had only been a few months since she found out."

The women silently shake their heads and think of their college friend, who was always full of life, vibrant, and ready to conquer the world.

"There is a site where we can make donations to the family," Collins shares without looking up from her phone.

"That's a great way for us to help. I am sure there are a lot of unexpected expenses to come," Jade responds, her practical side always taking the lead.

"I hadn't even considered the financial burden. Her poor kids and husband must be heartbroken. The emotional toll is enough to deal with," Elle says as her emotion causes her voice to crack.

Jade hands Elle a tissue.

"I'm sorry, I just can't imagine how difficult this must all be. And now I am thinking about our own mortality. You just never really know when something like this can happen to you," Elle says, continuing to blot her eyes.

"Nothing's going to happen to you," Collins asserts. "You worry too much. Here," she says, topping off Elle's wine.

"Collins," Jade probes, "you don't worry about this stuff?"

"Why would I? I can't control whether I'm going to get hit by a bus today or hit by cancer in forty years. I guess I prefer not to think about it," Collins states matter-of-factly.

"I prefer not to think about it too," Jade says. "But I think it is something we could be somewhat prepared for."

"Always one to have a plan," Collins jokes, looking to lighten the conversation.

"Absolutely," Jade fires back. "I want to make sure that I am in a good position financially if something happened to Logan. And I want you to be in a good position, too, if something were to happen to James."

For many people, like Collins, thinking about the what-ifs in life can be challenging. That's why in this chapter we're going to talk about ways that you can protect yourself and your family against financial losses that can come with the unexpected what-ifs that life can bring.

PROTECTION PROVIDES SECURITY

Life throws curveballs that can easily put you off balance. These events range from the minor—a basement flood, a car accident—to the major—a lawsuit, chronic illness, or death. The more layers of protection you have to insulate yourself against those curveballs, the better off you will be for two reasons. One, putting protection in place means that you won't have to worry as much about the financial what-if questions that pop up when life's unknowns occur. Two, when these things do happen—and they happen to all of us—having your finances already figured out will allow you to focus on your overall emotional and physical well-being. Having protections in place will make it easier for you and your family to navigate difficult circumstances with greater confidence.

THE MORE LAYERS OF PROTECTION YOU HAVE TO INSULATE YOURSELF AGAINST THOSE CURVEBALLS, THE BETTER OFF YOU WILL BE.

The first step in protecting yourself and your family is determining what you need to shield against losing. Emergency savings provide a cushion against some expenses, but other life events result in more catastrophic losses. When you have something to lose and you know that you could not afford to pay for a loss yourself, insurance provides a way for you to protect your lifestyle and assets. By paying a small amount of money each month, you can have the assurance that if something goes wrong, the insurance company will compensate you financially.

Deciding what types of protection you need largely depends on where you are in life, the kinds of assets you own, the liabilities you carry, and your long-term goals. Let's take a look at different types of insurance that can help you maintain financial empowerment.

PROTECT YOUR HEALTH

Health insurance protects you against medical emergencies and costly chronic health problems, a necessity for all. Even routine and preventive care can be expensive. Having insurance in place protects against these expenses too.

Understanding your out-of-pocket health insurance expenses is essential to be prepared for major medical events.

Premium: The amount you pay for insurance coverage regardless of receiving medical attention.

Copayment: The amount you pay at the time of service.

Deductible: The amount you pay *before* your insurance company starts to pay its share.

Coinsurance: The percentage of the costs you continue to pay *after* meeting your deductible until you reach the policy maximum.

Out-of-pocket maximum: The maximum amount you pay for medical costs in one year.

The cost structure of your insurance is driven by the type of plan. **Traditional health insurance plans** combine higher monthly premiums with lower deductibles and copayments to help spread out the insurance costs. The insurance company shares in all the medical expenses. **High-deductible health plans** have a lower monthly premium and higher deductibles. You are responsible for 100 percent of your medical expenses prior to meeting your deductible. Once you have met the deductible limit, the insurance company will start to share in the costs.

Your individual circumstances might make one of these options more attractive than the other. If you seek medical assistance frequently, have large medical expenses, or, like Elle and Collins, have small children, then traditional health insurance can be beneficial due to the lower deductible. If, like Jade, you are in good health, seek preventive care, and do not have children, then lower premiums with a higher deductible might be attractive. Participating in a high-deductible plan also allows Jade to contribute to a Health Savings Account.

If you and your partner each have employer-sponsored health plans, you may be eligible for benefits under dual coverage. This allows you to coordinate benefits when making insurance claims, which increases your overall coverage and can reduce your out-of-pocket costs. If you (and your children) are eligible to be covered under two insurance plans, discuss with your insurance providers how coordination of benefits would work for your circumstances.

If you do not have employer-sponsored health insurance, work with an insurance professional to become educated on individual-plan options available to you. Consider your physical and financial health when selecting a plan. Be cautious of defaulting to the lowest premium option unless you are able to pay for higher costs out of pocket until meeting your deductible.

EMPOWER TIP: Include vision and dental coverages when enrolling in your health insurance plan.

Regardless of the type of plan you have, it is important to understand the costs and future expenses that you could incur. Estimate the annual costs and know your maximum out-of-pocket expenses. I recommend factoring your out-of-pocket maximum into the amount you maintain in emergency savings. This will ensure that you are prepared for the costs that can arise from a major medical event.

> **EMPOWER TIP:** If you have a high-deductible health plan, maintain an HSA with a minimum balance equal to your annual deductible and ideally enough to cover your out-of-pocket maximum.

PROTECT YOUR INCOME

For most of us, our greatest asset is not our home or our retirement savings—it is our lifetime earning potential. Disability insurance helps you pay your bills when an unforeseen circumstance, such as an accident or illness, causes you to temporarily stop working. This is why disability insurance is important to consider when it comes to financial empowerment.

Short-term disability insurance can cover you if you are disabled for a short period of time (less than six months), and **long-term disability insurance** protects your income and helps you provide for your family should your disability persist for a period exceeding six months.

Like any other insurance, there are a lot of factors when considering which insurance coverage is right for you. The type of work you do is important. This will establish your occupation class, which is determined by the risk factors of your job. **Own occupation** insurance provides benefits if you are unable to perform the duties of your actual job, while **any occupation** provides coverage only if you are unable to perform the duties of any job you are qualified for.

The period between the occurrence of your disability and when your benefit would begin is important to consider; this is called the **elimination period**. The **benefit period**, how long you would be eligible to receive benefits, is also significant. A major disability could eliminate all your future earnings, so consider having coverage in place until your target retirement age.

Let's use Elle as an example. Should the unthinkable happen to her, with no disability coverage, losing income over even a short time period could have a ripple effect. If Elle were unable to work for six months, she would need to use half her emergency savings, $25,000. However, her loss would be greater than $25,000. Elle's emergency fund savings rate is $300 a month. If she had to spend half her emergency savings fund, it would take *seven years* to replenish it at her current rate *and* impact her ability to save for her other goals. This illustrates how disability insurance can help prevent a compounding financial hardship.

While James, Jade, and Logan all have short-term disability coverage through their employers, they do not have long-term coverage. The longer a disabling event lasts, the greater the impact to your financial empowerment. With most people depending heavily on their income for their livelihood, almost everyone should consider how disability insurance fits into their protection plan.

EMPOWER TIP: Inflation is an important consideration when looking at disability insurance. Look to have your benefits increase with the cost of inflation over time.

PROTECT YOUR LIFE

When it comes to life insurance, the majority of people are under-insured. Women are disproportionately underinsured, with women having lower coverage amounts and many not having coverage at all.[11] The amount of life insurance coverage you need depends largely on the financial needs of those who depend on you, the stage of your career and future earning power, the amount of debt and other assets you have, and your goals.

It is important that *all women* explore having some level of life insurance in place—regardless of career or marital status. Even someone with no children or spouse may want to consider life insurance to cover final expenses or create a legacy for other family members or charity. In determining how much life insurance is appropriate for you, start by outlining your and your partner's LIFE:

Liabilities

Income

Future goals

Expenses and estate taxes

The cash payout of life insurance proceeds offers instant financial relief, allowing your family access to funds for both short- and long-term expenses, such as funeral and burial costs, final debts, medical bills, and paying off a mortgage. Income replacement allows your family to continue to cover day-to-day expenses without stress. Additionally, money from life insurance policies can be set aside for anticipated future expenses associated with your goals, such as education or retirement. For larger estates it can be earmarked to pay estate taxes as well as legacy and charitable planning.

> **EMPOWER TIP:** Life insurance can be used to protect assets, provide for your family, build wealth, and support estate planning.

Types of Insurance

Outlining your LIFE will also help you identify the duration of your insurance needs, which will help determine what type of life insurance is needed. **Term insurance** allows you to "rent" protection for a set period of time, typically thirty years or less. With **permanent insurance**, you "own" a policy designed to cover your whole life.

For the years you have children at home, high-earning years, or to cover outstanding liabilities, such as a mortgage, you might be interested in lower-cost term insurance. If you find that you have a more permanent need for protection, goals, a legacy, or estate taxes, you may consider whole life, universal life, variable universal life, or indexed universal life insurance. While permanent insurance has a higher cost, the cost varies depending on the different features a policy provides. Premiums can be fixed or flexible, death benefits can be guaranteed or adjustable, and cash value can accumulate based on interest or investments.

Choosing the coverage that is right for you depends on several factors, including your age, health, budget, and policy features. In many cases, a combination of term and permanent life insurance can be the best solution to protect your family's financial future. Working with an experienced insurance agent can help you fine-tune the amount and type of insurance that is right for you.

Like so many other women, our investors find themselves uncertain about their life insurance needs. The LIFE exercise has helped them consider how much insurance they need and what type of insurance is most appropriate. Elle has a small $10,000 policy through her employer, but she realizes that if something were to happen to her, she would need and want to provide much more for Ava. She wants to consider a larger term policy to cover the years until Ava gets through college and a smaller permanent policy that would pay out to Ava later in life as part of her legacy planning.

The exercise raises questions for Collins. She recognizes that they need more coverage for the children's earlier years, but how much money would she need beyond that? While they have life insurance through James's employer—$900,000 on James and $100,000 on Collins—the coverage for James, as the primary income earner for their family, is not nearly enough. And what would happen if he were to get a new job? Would he have the same amount of insurance with a different employer?

Jade and Logan each have two times their salary provided in group insurance through their employers. Additionally, they have term insurance policies that provide coverage to age sixty, $500,000 for Jade and $750,000 for Logan. While she feels good about the coverage they have in place to age sixty, she wonders whether they should consider more permanent coverage to help address how to handle the "mine" and "yours" nature of their assets. If one of them passes away before the other, how will that impact the survivor's lifestyle in retirement?

PROTECT YOUR PROPERTY

There are other areas of your life where it is important to have appropriate protection in place. Property and casualty insurance is a smart investment that can help you and your family in the event of an unforeseen accident in your home or on your property.

Your **homeowner's insurance** should provide you with compensation for financial losses including the cost of repairing or rebuilding your house (dwelling value); the value of replacing the contents of your home, including personal property; the cost of additional living expenses during a repair or rebuild; and personal liability to protect your assets. If, like Elle, you are not a homeowner, then **renters' insurance** will cover replacing personal property, additional living expenses, and liability if you are responsible for damage or injury.

Just as you insure where you live, you also want to maintain suitable car insurance. Your **auto insurance** policy should include property damage, collision, comprehensive, bodily injury, uninsured motorist, and personal injury protection.

> **EMPOWER TIP:** If you have a loan on your car, make sure your auto insurance will pay off the full loan value.

Personal liability coverage is another area where people are likely to be underinsured. An umbrella insurance policy can be used as a secondary form of insurance that is triggered after policy limits are reached in your home and auto policies. Collins and James carry $1 million in umbrella insurance, an additional layer of protection in an instance when an accident or catastrophic event could result in injury, property damage, and certain lawsuits. As a landlord, Jade finds it to be relatively inexpensive for the added insulation it provides and carries $1 million of personal liability coverage.

REVIEW YOUR INSURANCE PROTECTION

As for so many of us, having someone they know experience a life-altering event has caused our investors to contemplate the impact such an event would have on their lives. As they reviewed the insurance protection they have in place, they uncovered areas where they are potentially exposed.

Elle recognizes that she is underinsured in many areas. She will look into additional life insurance, disability insurance, and an umbrella policy to create greater financial security for her and Ava.

As they work on setting their goals, Collins and James will revisit the coverage they have in place for disability and life insurance. Collins doesn't know much about their financial situation, but she does know that $900,000 is insufficient to cover income replacement, future goals, and a legacy for their children if James were to pass away. They will also consider whether $1 million of extra liability coverage is sufficient, given their growing net worth and two children that will quickly become teenagers.

Jade and Logan will examine the impact a loss of income due to disability during their working years would have on their overall financial picture. They will also inquire about eligibility for domestic partner coverage on each other's health insurance plans to coordinate benefits. Thinking beyond their working years, they will outline a strategy for individual healthcare until age sixty-five and the ramifications of their term life insurance expiring at age sixty.

IT IS IMPORTANT TO REVIEW YOUR INSURANCE NEEDS, NOW AND AS PART OF YOUR ANNUAL FINANCIAL HEALTH CHECK.

It is important to review your insurance needs, now and as part of your annual financial health check. As your circumstances change, so will your needs. Make sure you understand what your policies cover and, more importantly, where gaps in protection may exist. Having proper protection is critical to your and your family's confidence in your journey to financial empowerment.

PROTECT YOUR LEGACY

Beyond insurance, legal planning should be completed to protect you and your family, as well as your assets, in the case of death or incapacity. As we overheard our investors discuss, there is a lot of fear and anxiety wrapped up in these topics. But planning well can mitigate these emotions and give you the confidence that you and your loved ones are prepared for the future, no matter what it may bring.

Estate Planning

Estate planning is the process of determining what will happen if you die or become incapacitated. It covers who would make decisions for you if you were unable to make them for yourself, your financial wishes both during your lifetime and when you are ultimately gone, and, if applicable, who would become the guardian of your children. Everyone should complete an estate plan. Creating a plan to communicate your wishes and provide for your loved ones will allow you to have greater control and confidence.

A **simple will** outlines who will inherit your property and assets when you die, how they will receive them, and who is responsible for facilitating the process of transferring property and assets from your estate to those individuals. For most people the hardest part of the planning is determining the following:

Executor: Whom to put in charge of carrying out your wishes

Legal guardian: Whom you want to care for your children

Beneficiaries: Whom you want to receive your belongings and assets

Even those who feel like the answers are obvious should still complete a simple will. It communicates your wishes not only to your loved ones but also to the courts. Those who do not have a will at the time of death are at the mercy of the state, with courts determining the answers to the above questions for you.

Probate is the legal process that allows the courts to verify the legality of your will, inventory your property and outstanding liabilities, and enable your executor to move forward with executing your will. For women, like Jade, in nontraditional relationships, having proper estate planning is vital. Even though she and Logan have been partners for thirteen years, without legal documentation, the court could rule that she has no rights in regard to his estate.

A **living will** is a written set of legally binding instructions for your physician outlining any life-sustaining measures you would want if you became terminally ill or permanently unconscious. This document, along with a health proxy, allows you to appoint an individual to carry out your wishes when you cannot do so yourself. For Elle, like other single women, this allows her to appoint someone to make healthcare-related decisions, based on her documented wishes, in the event that she becomes incapacitated.

A **durable power of attorney** enables you to designate a trusted individual to take over the responsibility of financial decision-making, if needed. This person serves as your financial advocate, ensuring the decisions they make are in your best interest. Having this planning in place will be critical for Jade and Logan. Since they hold their assets separately, this document will enable them to access each other's accounts if they were to become unable to access them on their own.

One of the most challenging parts of estate planning is exploring the difficult what-if scenarios we heard our investors walk through at the beginning of this chapter. This includes making decisions about who would care for your children if the unthinkable happens. Beyond selecting the individual whom you know will love and care for them, there is an opportunity to document your legacy. You are your child's most important asset. You are the walking encyclopedia of their experiences, history, wishes, and habits. Consider using a **letter of intent** to communicate this valuable information, as well as your wishes for their future, to them and their guardian. Revisit and update your letter every year as your child grows.

While basic estate planning addresses all of Elle's and Collins's concerns, Jade finds that her relationship status may result in a need for more complex planning. Advanced estate planning typically involves more layers to navigate and potentially trusts to achieve your planning objectives. **Trusts** are commonly used in circumstances that include a blended family, a beneficiary who has special needs, and property owned in multiple states, as well as for estates in excess of estate tax exclusion amounts. If your estate includes complexities, work with a specialized attorney to execute appropriate planning for your estate and financial goals.

EMPOWER TIP: Be sure to consider taxes when completing your estate planning. The federal government, as well as twelve states, levies taxes on estates exceeding certain thresholds.

Jade is anxious to learn more about how to structure her estate planning. With her and Logan keeping their finances separate, she wants her assets to go to Logan during his lifetime but ultimately to pass to her family members if they are still living at the end of his life. She wonders whether they will need to explore advanced estate planning or whether they can accomplish their desired outcome with strategic account titling and beneficiary designations.

TITLES AND DESIGNATIONS

When it comes to your financial accounts, names are *really* important. How accounts are titled determines the legal ownership of the asset. The best estate plans can be undone if you do not title assets correctly. This is true for bank accounts, investment accounts, property, and any other item that requires **legal titling**.

You want to coordinate your asset titling with your overall estate plan. Pay attention to jointly titled assets, as there are many ways those assets can be titled—**joint tenants**, **tenants in common**, **tenants by entirety**, and **community property** being a few. Each has its own advantages and disadvantages. Your planning professionals will help determine how to title your assets to be consistent with your overall plan and wishes.

It is also important to note whether you live in a state that has community property rules. In nine states, assets and debt acquired during marriage are considered part of the "community" and deemed to be owned fifty-fifty, regardless of how they are titled. Inherited assets are exempt from community property rules and can be owned individually, assuming they are not commingled with joint assets. Maintaining these assets separately can be empowering and contribute to stronger financial confidence.

> **EMPOWER TIP:** Titling inherited assets as separate property allows you to retain sole ownership and control of those assets in the future.

With careful planning, **beneficiary designations** can be a powerful estate planning tool, allowing assets to pass to beneficiaries without going through your estate. This can be helpful in streamlining the process of settling an estate and can allow for more efficient tax management on taxable assets. If an account has a beneficiary tied to it, that asset will pass directly to those beneficiaries, regardless of what you stipulated in your will. That's right: your beneficiary designations supersede your will, making beneficiary designations a key component to your estate planning.

A **beneficiary** can be an individual, a trust, or an entity. By listing a beneficiary, you are documenting who, or what, will become the legal owner of your asset when you pass away. Retirement accounts, pensions, annuities, and life insurance allow you to list primary and contingent beneficiaries. Beneficiaries can be added to other accounts by making them **payable on death (POD)** if they are bank accounts or **transfer on death (TOD)** if they are brokerage accounts.

Depending on the state where you live, you may also be able to list a beneficiary to inherit your vehicle registration or deed to your real estate. Beneficiary designations should not be made lightly, and you should consider your long-term goals when determining which beneficiaries to designate. Due to the legally binding nature of beneficiaries, you should review them every year and update after any major life events, including marriage, the birth of children or grandchildren, divorce, and death.[12]

EMPOWER TIP: Review your beneficiaries every year when you complete your taxes to make sure they are up to date.

Jade and Logan currently list each other as their **primary beneficiaries** on their retirement accounts but can add their own siblings as their contingent beneficiaries. **Contingent beneficiaries** are secondary beneficiaries, to whom an asset passes if the primary beneficiary is deceased or disclaims it. By adding her siblings as contingent beneficiaries, Jade ensures that, if Logan were to predecease her, the money would go to her siblings at her passing. Without contingent beneficiaries, the assets would go into her estate and be distributed through the probate process.

BE PROACTIVE

After you establish an estate plan—whether it's basic or advanced—review your documents to make sure they are current and accurate. Check your assets to confirm that your titling and, if applicable, beneficiary designations support your estate planning documents. When you make changes to your estate plans, carry those changes through to your account titling and beneficiary designations. It's critical to maintain the most up-to-date copy of your estate planning documents in a secure location along with your other essential documents. These documents are commonly stored in a safe or safe-deposit box. Make sure that your loved ones know where they are kept and how to access the documents.

> **EMPOWER TIP:** Courts usually require original documents. Keep important documents in a safe and secure place where they cannot be misplaced or damaged by water or fire.

The emotional nature of this subject matter means that we often put it off for as long as possible. The reality is it is a key step in building financial empowerment. Our investors, like many of us, need to prioritize getting their estate planning documents up to date.

Elle and her ex-husband, Ethan, completed estate planning documents when they found out she was pregnant with Ava. While she removed Ethan from her account titles and beneficiary designations after the divorce, she has not updated her simple and living wills. She also had not considered a letter of intent. She likes the idea of Ava having a letter from her if she were gone. There is so much that she would want her to know: how much she loves her and all that she hopes she will discover in the life that lies ahead. Elle has a safe-deposit box where she stores her estate planning documents along with her and Ava's other essential documents—birth certificates, Social Security cards, marriage and divorce documentation, and her last three years of tax returns.

Like Elle, Collins created a will when Hayes was born, but she and James have not reviewed their planning in the past six years. They had a difficult time agreeing on who would be his guardian, both wanting their own family members to step in. They ultimately agreed that it should be Collins's brother and sister-in-law, but by the time they finally got to that point, she had forgotten all about completing a letter of intent. Their planning was completed before Harper was born, and they have not updated any of the documents to include her. Collins wants to review the documents to see how they accounted for any future children, but she will first need to locate them. They do not have a central location for storing their important documents. Collins will have to search through all the files in the study—another opportunity to get their affairs organized! She wants to review the titling of their assets to confirm their joint assets are titled appropriately and add the children as contingent beneficiaries on James's retirement account and their life insurance policies.

Surprisingly, estate planning is the one area of finances where Jade does not have a plan. Having separate finances has always given her confidence that she would be okay if she needed to go out on her own. But she realizes that having proper planning in place is important for their financial lives, living or deceased. Since she and Logan are not married, they want to appoint each other as the decision maker for any health and financial matters while living and determine the best way to structure their assets so they can support each other in the case of death. They ultimately want their assets to pass to their respective families. Both Jade and Logan will update their beneficiary designations to include their family members as contingent and make changes after completing their planning if necessary. Jade will also review all the essential documents stored in their safe to make sure that everything they need is there, including online credentials for both of them. If something were to happen to Logan, she would not know where to begin with trying to access any of his online accounts. Estate planning jumps to the top of Jade's priority list. She realizes that her current circumstances leave her with a lot of question marks when considering life's what-ifs.

THE MORE YOU PREPARE FOR UNEXPECTED LIFE EVENTS, THE MORE CONFIDENT YOU WILL BE NAVIGATING CHALLENGING TIMES WHEN THEY OCCUR.

TAKE ACTION!

Life is sprinkled with unknowns that can fill us with worry. The more you prepare for unexpected life events, the more confident you will be navigating challenging times when they occur. Having proper protection in place is a vital aspect of financial empowerment. As challenging as it can be, it is necessary to **ENVISION** the protection you and your family need.

E   **EMPOWER** yourself by understanding your circumstances and preparing for the unexpected.

N   **NARROW** your focus by identifying the protection you and your family need.

V   **VALIDATE** that you have proper protection in place to safeguard yourself and your family.

I   **IMPLEMENT** your estate planning by verifying that your account titles and beneficiaries align with your planning.

S   **SHARE** your wishes and where to find your important documents with your loved ones.

I   **INCENTIVIZE** yourself to complete all facets of your protection planning.

O   **OVERSEE** proper execution by partnering with professionals who have experience in insurance and estate planning.

N   **NAVIGATE** life by reviewing your protection annually, and update when major life events occur.

CHAPTER FIVE

INVESTOR ESSENTIALS

November

As Collins wiggles out of her coat and Jade hands her a cocktail, Collins, bursting with excitement, announces, "I'm an investor!"

Jade smiles. "Which designer bag is it this time?"

"Not a bag," Collins says.

"Shoes, then?" asks Elle. Like Jade, Elle is used to admiring Collins's "investments," which are attached to either her arm or her feet.

"You two are hilarious," Collins says. "As it happens, my investing *is* shopping related. I just bought a hundred shares of my favorite retail store," she tells them proudly. "I looked at where I spend all of my money, and since I can't get out of there without spending a few hundred dollars, I thought, 'Why not invest?'"

"I love it," says Jade. "Invest in what you know."

"I don't know what is more shocking," says Elle, "that you know how to buy a stock or the fact that you're watching your spending."

"Truth be told, James did the research and bought the stock, but

I made the suggestion."

"You deserve the credit," Jade says. "The fact that you even thought about the opportunity shows how far you've come. Maybe I should ask James for advice on my retirement account. I glance at the statements, and it seems to mostly go up, but I'm not sure how much of that is from the investments or the money I am continually adding," Jade admits.

"I should ask him too," Elle says. "I have money invested in CDs at the bank, but the interest that I earn is next to nothing."

"What's wrong with us?" Collins's face sours. "We are smart, educated women, and we're talking about asking my husband to help us with investments. Is he really more qualified to invest than we are?"

The apprehension that Collins, Jade, and Elle have about investing is all too common, especially among women. Investing can be perceived as complex and full of industry jargon, and for the inexperienced, it can feel intimidating. But, like any new thing, once you learn a little about the foundations of investing, you will develop enough confidence to invest on your own.[13]

WHY YOU SHOULD INVEST

Investing can increase your net worth faster than savings alone, making your money work for you. Investing is not simply about the pursuit of wealth; it's about giving yourself a tool for creating life choices. Remember, choice is a major component of financial empowerment.

It is essential to understand that investing is a long-term game—investors think in decades, not quarters. The goal for individual investors is to beat inflation and earn higher returns *over time*. Money in the bank provides security and liquidity, two things that are important for short-term goals, but only a minimal rate of return. Mid- and long-term goals typically need additional time to accumulate the money necessary to achieve them. If that money can earn a higher rate of return, the money will grow faster, making it easier to progress toward your goals. Depending on how long the time horizon is, investing—in the stock market for example—could potentially double or triple your earnings compared to what the same amount of money would be making at the bank. So, the question becomes, why would you *not* invest?

INVESTING IS NOT SIMPLY ABOUT THE PURSUIT OF WEALTH; IT'S ABOUT GIVING YOURSELF A TOOL FOR CREATING LIFE CHOICES.

WHEN YOU SHOULD INVEST

The earlier you start investing, the sooner you can take advantage of the power of compounding. The more time that you have for your investments to grow, the better off you will be. That's the concept of time value of money: investing a dollar today will benefit you more than investing a dollar in the future.

Investing is not meant to be an immediate way to increase your net worth. With investment returns varying year to year and even day to day, it is important to make sure that you have enough time on your side to recover any potential loss in value. Consider the time horizon and objectives of your goals before using investments to leverage the funds.

Generally, the closer you are to your goal, the less risk you want to take with the money you have accumulated. When you anticipate needing money for short-term goals, the primary objectives are preservation and accessibility. Finding the right balance of investments for midterm goals can be challenging, as it can be harder to identify when exactly you will achieve them. For midterm goals you want a balance of growth and protection. Long-term goals allow for a more aggressive investment strategy. The longer you have until you foresee needing the money, the more comfortable you can be focusing on growth.

Over time, your long-term goals will shift to midterm and ultimately to short term. With these shifts, your objectives will move from growth to balance to preservation. As the objectives of your goals change, so should your investment strategy.

WHERE YOU SHOULD INVEST

Whether you are new to investing or have been investing for years, you likely are familiar with the "markets." Let's explore what that really means and break down ways you can invest to gain exposure to them.

THE MARKETS

Billions of shares of stock change hands every day, a number that is too high for even seasoned Wall Street professionals to keep track of. This is why you frequently hear about the performance of the "stock market" as a whole. The three main indexes that are used as broad gauges for US stock performance are the Dow Jones Industrial Average (Dow), the Standard & Poor's 500 (S&P 500), and the NASDAQ Composite Index (Nasdaq).

The **Dow** is a price-weighted index of thirty large US companies, with high-priced stocks causing the index to move more than stocks with lower prices. The index is considered a good measure for blue-chip stocks—mature, stable, and recognizable companies with established histories. With only thirty companies included in the index, it is limited in how much of the overall market it represents.

The **S&P 500** is a market capitalization–weighted index, measuring the performance of five hundred of the largest US companies, with weight determined by a company's share price and number of outstanding shares. Tracking a larger pool of companies makes it a better gauge for large US companies.

The **Nasdaq** is also a market capitalization–weighted index that tracks all the stocks and securities that trade on the Nasdaq exchange: more than three thousand securities. It covers more companies than the other two indexes but tilts heavily toward technology and internet-related companies, resulting in a representation of growth companies versus the broad market.

Beyond these main indexes, there are many others that can be used to track specific segments of financial markets. Notably, the **Bloomberg Barclays US Aggregate Bond Index (Agg)**[14] is the most common benchmark for the US investment-grade bond market, while the performance of global markets is frequently tracked using the **MSCI All Country World Index (ACWI)**.[15]

While these indexes can indicate how segments of financial markets are generally moving, they include only small fractions of investments. Indexes can be useful tools in monitoring broad performance, but keep in mind that your investments are likely not moving completely in step with these market gauges. Most of us do not hold investments that are identical to those in these indexes[16] and therefore should not expect stock market–like returns. This applies to both the upside and the downside. While it can be easy to get caught up in the news of the markets, it is important not to fixate on short-term movements when you are investing for goals with longer time horizons.

TYPES OF INVESTMENTS

At their most basic level, investments fall into three categories: stocks, bonds, and cash. Stocks are ownership shares, bonds are debt instruments, and cash includes assets that can be readily converted to cash without risking loss of value.

STOCKS

Stocks represent an equity ownership in a company. Once you purchase a share of stock, you have a stake in the company's growth and profits. When a company performs well, its stock tends to increase in value, and if a company underperforms, so will its stock. The risk of owning a stock is that the value of your shares is directly tied to the performance of a single company and other investors' desire to own shares of that company. The price of stock can change from second to second during market trading hours depending on how many investors are buying versus selling shares. When there are more investors looking to buy than sell shares of a company, the price will increase. The price will decrease when more investors are selling than buying shares. It is basic supply and demand. This results in stocks experiencing greater volatility than other investments; they tend to have larger swings in value in the short term, which is why it is wise to include them as part of your *long-term* investment strategy.

Stocks are typically categorized by **size** (how much a company is worth based on the number of outstanding shares and share price) and **style** (how the company is expected to maximize value). Where a company falls in these categories helps investors assess the risk of the investment. For size, the risk decreases with the number of outstanding shares. **Large-cap** companies have $10 billion or more in outstanding shares, **mid-cap** companies have $2 to $10 billion, and

small-cap companies have less than $2 billion.

Style primarily encompasses value and growth. **Value stocks** frequently pay dividends from profits, providing cash flow that can be reinvested or used to cover income needs. These stocks tend to have lower risk and may trade at lower prices. **Growth stocks** have growing earnings and profits. They are expected to increase in value more quickly, resulting in a share price that can be higher than current earnings. Growth stocks do not typically pay dividends; the companies reinvest their profits in the growing business. These stocks tend to have higher risk, may trade at higher prices, and have the greatest upside potential.

Let's look at Jade's mid- and long-term goals to see how different sizes and styles of stocks can fit into her investment strategy. Because she has plans to purchase an investment property in three to five years, dividend-paying large-cap stocks would be more suitable for investing those funds. The returns from stable companies will be more moderate compared to growth companies that have higher potential returns but also higher risk. Growth stocks (including large, mid-, and small cap) would be more appropriate in her retirement account, where the time horizon is more than ten years away.

Additionally, she can look to add **international stock** exposure, including both developed and emerging markets, in her long-term retirement savings. Just as there are different types of risk in different US stocks, it is important to understand the different risks in this category.[17] The term **developed markets** refers to countries with established, mature economies and capital markets, like North America, western Europe, Hong Kong, Japan, and Australia. These countries have greater stability and therefore less risk. **Emerging markets** are countries that are still developing, with more potential for rapid growth. Brazil, Russia, India, China, and South Africa are countries with economies that are considered emerging. While there is a major opportunity for growth, the risk is higher due to factors including political environment, unstable currencies, and lack of regulations. With a higher risk/reward profile, international stocks carry a tremendous amount of volatility. Jade is interested in higher return potential, but she should be cautious about investing too much of her allocation into high-risk asset classes.

> **EMPOWER TIP:** Risk exists at varying levels within each category of stocks. Consider the risk of each investment holding carefully to understand how it contributes to your overall risk tolerance.

BONDS

While stocks are an important tool for growth, investors look to bonds to balance the risk of stocks. Rather than owning a share of a company, investors lend money to a company or government entity (**issuer**). The issuer determines the total amount it wants to borrow (**issue size**) and breaks that into individual bonds to be sold to investors. The issuer promises to repay the borrowed amount (**par value**) after a specific period of time (**maturity date**) and pay a fixed interest rate (**yield**) to the investor during the borrowing period.

Bonds are also referred to as fixed income. Having a fixed period and fixed interest makes bonds more stable than stocks. While stocks are purchased for their upside potential, bonds are purchased for their predictability, which equates to lower return potential. Lower risk, lower reward. The same supply and demand principles that apply to stocks apply to bonds if you are going to trade them on the open market. However, since bonds carry less risk, they are less volatile, making them a great tool to preserve capital, create predictable cash flow, and reduce portfolio volatility.

EMPOWER TIP: Bonds are loans, like an IOU, with set interest and repayment terms.

While bonds are a more conservative investment option, they are not risk-free. Like stocks, the type of bonds you invest in should be based on your risk tolerance, time frame, and objectives.

There are two main categories for bond issuers: **government** (US Treasury and municipal bonds) and **corporate** bonds. Bonds issued by the US Treasury are considered the lowest risk because the federal government is deemed to be the most creditworthy issuer, or the least likely to default. **Default risk** measures the probability an issuer will be able to make interest and principal payments, satisfying the obligation.

> THE TYPE OF BONDS YOU INVEST IN SHOULD BE BASED ON YOUR RISK TOLERANCE, TIME FRAME, AND OBJECTIVES.

In order to know the financial strength of a bond issuer, rating agencies assign a **credit risk** rating to each bond issue, similar to a credit score, based on the issuer's creditworthiness. The lower the credit rating, the higher the risk of default. The relationship between risk and reward of course still holds true. Bonds with higher credit ratings (US Treasury and investment-grade bonds) pay lower yields than bonds with lower credit ratings. The lowest-rated bonds are referred to as high yield, as they pay the highest interest rates.

Changes in prevailing interest rates will impact the value of bonds.

Having an inverse relationship with interest rates, bond prices will fall when interest rates rise and rise when interest rates fall. A bond's level of sensitivity to changes in interest rates is measured by **duration**. Bonds with a higher duration would be expected to decrease more when overall interest rates rise. Investors can mitigate **interest rate risk** by owning bonds with varying maturities.

The risk and reward relationship between interest rates and maturities is illustrated in yield curves. A normal yield curve will be upward sloping, with longer maturities paying higher yields than credit-equivalent bonds with shorter maturities. The extra return received in the form of higher yields is how investors are compensated for longer time to maturity, higher duration, and greater interest rate risk. Short-term bonds have less risk and are preferred by those seeking stability and therefore willing to forgo higher yields.

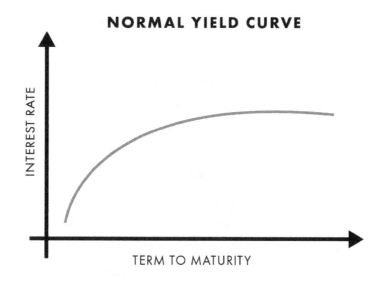

Source: "What is the Yield Curve?," Corporate Finance Institute, https://corporatefinanceinstitute.com/resources/knowledge/finance/yield-curve/.

Yield curves are important because they give insight into what investors expect to earn in the future. The shape of the curve is influenced by the outlook for economic growth, inflation, and interest rates. A **normal yield curve** indicates stable or expanding economic conditions. If the yield curve shifts to a **flat yield curve**, it means there is economic uncertainty, and if it shifts to slope downward (**inverted yield curve**), investors expect lower returns in the long term, signaling an economic downturn. Even if you do not heavily invest in bonds, the yield curve is an important indicator of what is expected to impact the economy and various investment vehicles.

CASH

There may be instances when investors want to protect principal with even less risk than the most conservative bonds. Cash and cash equivalents are ideal for short-term goals. They are high credit quality and typically your most liquid asset. Elle has historically kept all her money in assets that fall into cash investments, money market funds, or certificates of deposit (CDs), drawn to the stable value of these investments. The money she puts in these accounts does not decrease in value unless she makes a withdrawal. While the interest she earns is low, so is the risk. **Inflation risk** is the primary risk of cash investments. Inflation reduces buying power over time. Ideally you want your money to grow at a faster pace than the rising costs of goods and services. Since cash has the lowest investment return, it can be difficult for bank money to keep up with increasing costs.

EMPOWER TIP: Inflation erodes the purchasing power of money over time. Make sure your cash earns the highest interest rate available to combat inflation.

Acknowledging that too many of her investments fall into this asset category, Elle decides that she is ready to take on investing outside of cash. She likes the idea of bonds and value stocks but feels overwhelmed by all the moving parts and the number of options. While stocks and bonds are the most basic ways that companies and government entities allow investments, there are clearly a lot of factors to consider before investing. Fortunately, there are investment vehicles that allow investors to gain broad exposure to numerous stocks and bonds with a single holding. Our investors look to better understand the mechanics of mutual funds and exchange-traded funds (ETFs).

MUTUAL FUNDS

Mutual funds pool stocks, bonds, and other securities in a single investment vehicle. The value of the mutual fund shares rises and falls with the value of the underlying holdings.[18] An advantage to mutual fund investors is that they own a small slice of each of the stock and bond holdings. A single mutual fund share represents an investment in anywhere from a dozen to several hundred different investments.

The mutual fund universe is vast. You can narrow your focus starting with the fund investment type—stocks, bonds, or multi-asset. **Stock mutual funds** are typically broken down by what type of companies they invest in (large, mid-, and small cap) and what the primary objective of the fund is (growth, value, or both). **Bond mutual funds** can be categorized by type of issuer, time to maturity, and credit risk. **Multi-asset mutual funds** blend both stocks and bonds to achieve target allocations. Beyond investment type, mutual funds can be differentiated according to their management approach (active or passive), industry, sector, index, or geographical region.

> **EMPOWER TIP:** Mutual funds are a great way to start investing. It takes only a handful of mutual funds to build a well-diversified portfolio.

Many resources are available to help you identify a mutual fund's investment objective, risk profile, and history. The mutual fund summary or fact sheet will state the fund's investment objective. The risk of a mutual fund depends on the underlying holdings of the mutual fund. This information can be found by looking up the mutual fund's overview and examining the fund's style box. The style box illustrates the categories of the fund holdings for both stocks (size and style) and bonds (credit and duration). Use the style box, combined with investment objectives, to narrow your investment options based on your risk tolerance. From there you may want to compare mutual fund track records by looking at historical performance as well as Morningstar ratings.

Mutual funds are a great option for our investors, who are looking to simplify the investment process. Mutual funds make it easy to invest in a broad range of holdings, with the fund manager doing most of the heavy lifting. Their role is to research the underlying holdings, manage those holdings on an ongoing basis, and handle all the administration for investors.

There is, of course, a cost for these services, which is annual-percentage **operating expense**. When looking at mutual fund companies and specific mutual funds, consider the level of active management relative to these ongoing expenses. Additionally, there are **shareholder fees**, which include up-front costs of investing as well as ongoing fees for trading and account maintenance. All expenses associated with a mutual fund are listed in the fund prospectus.[19]

Elle narrows her focus to **age-based** and **target-date** funds,[20] which will allow her to set a date for when she anticipates starting to withdraw the money from her investments. The fund manager automatically adjusts the investments at set intervals, reducing the risk as the age or date grows closer. While Jade feels she has a good understanding of mutual funds, she wants to understand how they compare to exchange-traded funds.

EXCHANGE-TRADED FUNDS

Exchange-traded funds (ETFs) are baskets of securities that offer the diversification benefits of mutual funds combined with a stock's ease of trading. While there are some actively managed ETFs, the majority are passive and track an underlying broad market index (such as the S&P 500), market sector (such as technology), or commodity (such as gold). In general, investors look to ETFs over mutual funds for their stock-trading feature, lower costs, and greater control of taxable events. Passive ETFs buy and hold securities, resulting in greater tax efficiency and lower expense ratios than mutual funds. While these traits may be beneficial to some, others find that the broader objectives and greater management of mutual funds are a better fit for their investment needs.[21]

Our investors will primarily use mutual funds to become more comfortable with investing. Ultimately, their confidence and investment knowledge will increase, and they will explore investing with ETFs and individual securities for greater efficiency and cost savings. When they have strong convictions, they will invest in specific companies, as Collins did at the beginning of the chapter. This mixed approach is a great way to get a feel for how investing works and see how different investment vehicles perform over time.

HOW TO START INVESTING

Hopefully you are starting to gain a better understanding of your investment options and, like our investors, feel ready to take the next step. The goals that you set in chapter 1 will help you determine which type of investment account you want to use. Most of us have retirement as a long-term goal, which makes retirement accounts one of the most obvious places to start investing. If you work for an employer that provides an employer-sponsored retirement plan, the plan has already done some of the work by narrowing down your investment options and monitoring those options to ensure they meet their stated objective. If you are not participating in your employer's retirement plan, take steps to enroll today.

Jade utilizes her employer's 401(k) plan for her retirement savings. She contributes $500 each pay period, which is automatically invested. By systematically investing every two weeks, regardless of price, she benefits from **dollar-cost averaging**.[22] This allows her to buy more shares when the price of the fund is down and fewer shares when the price is high, eliminating emotional investing and potentially reducing **market risk**.

If your employer, like Elle's, does not offer a retirement plan or, like Collins, you are not currently working but your spouse is, establish an IRA with a mutual fund company or online brokerage firm. In addition to retirement, consider what other investment accounts would be suitable for your savings goals. Elle, who is excited to systematically invest her monthly savings, establishes both a Roth IRA and 529 college savings account with a mutual fund company.

For midterm and long-term goals outside of retirement and college savings, consider setting up an after-tax investment account. Collins and James have a joint brokerage account where he has invested in stocks and mutual funds. While they have not tied a specific goal to this account, they have the flexibility to access the funds at any time, making it a great resource for midterm goals and any future goals they have yet to identify.

> **EMPOWER TIP:** Start investing today. Begin with a minimum amount to get your feet wet and watch how your investments move.

ASSET ALLOCATION

Asset allocation is one of the biggest factors in determining your long-term financial success. Investing in different asset classes (stocks,

ASSET ALLOCATION IS ONE OF THE BIGGEST FACTORS IN DETERMINING YOUR LONG-TERM FINANCIAL SUCCESS.

bonds, and cash) ensures that you do not have all your eggs in one basket, providing **diversification**[23] that helps to maintain balance and mitigate risk. If you invest in several asset classes and securities, your return will depend on the average of those classes' investment returns versus the sole performance of a single asset class or investment. This can lead to more consistent returns, which will allow you to stay on track and focused on your goals. To diversify their investments, our investors will do the following:

- Use the time horizon of their goals to drive the level of risk that is most appropriate. In some instances they may start with lower risk and increase over time, but they will avoid taking more risk than necessary.

- Determine how much to invest in each asset class, based on their risk tolerance, beginning with the most conservative (cash) and working up to the most aggressive (stocks).

- Consider the risk of investments within each asset class. Do they want to own value or growth stocks? Investment-grade or high-yield bonds? Developed or emerging markets?

- Once they have identified their overall asset allocation, they will establish a personal benchmark based on the expected returns of their mix of assets, on average, over time.

Like our investors, you should evaluate your risk tolerance, determine an appropriate asset allocation, and set a personal benchmark. Personal benchmarks serve as the annual rate of return you will target for your investments. This enables you to set a metric that will allow you to make projections for your goal timeline and measure your progress annually to determine whether you are on track. Let's see what risk tolerance, asset allocations, and personal benchmarks our investors set:

Elle = Moderate Conservative

5 percent cash, 45 percent bonds, and 50 percent stocks
Personal benchmark target: 5 percent

Jade = Moderate

5 percent cash, 35 percent bonds, and 60 percent stocks
Personal benchmark target: 6 percent

Collins = Moderate Growth

30 percent bonds and 70 percent stocks
Personal benchmark target: 7 percent

Target allocations can change and should be reviewed at least annually. You may need to make adjustments due to life events, changes in time horizon, and investment performance. For example, Jade invests 60 percent of her 401(k) in stock mutual fund holdings. If those holdings perform well over a couple of years, she may find that the percentage she holds in stocks has increased to 70 percent, which is higher than she intended. To resolve this, she can simply **rebalance**[24] by moving the 10 percent excess in stock holdings to her other holdings. Rebalance as your investments grow, objectives shift, and goals change or when major life changes trigger a desire to decrease, or increase, your risk exposure.

> **EMPOWER TIP:** Maintaining accurate asset allocation will help you stay in control of your goals and make you a more confident investor.

HOW TO STAY INVESTED

Research shows the average investor will miss out on returns due to poor timing of investment decisions.[25] This is largely because investors frequently make irrational decisions driven by emotions, which can negatively impact their progress working toward their goals.

Have you ever heard the investment adage "Buy low, sell high"? This simply states that the most optimal way to invest is to buy when the investment price is low and sell when it appreciates to a high point. Great in theory, difficult in reality. In fact, most of us do the opposite. When the value of our investments goes up, we are filled with excitement and euphoria that it will continue to go up, so we stay invested. When the value of our investments declines rapidly, we are filled with a feeling of fear, panic, and despondency. This psychological phenomenon, the **cycle of investor emotions**, can drive us to make illogical decisions, frequently selling at the least opportune time.

Clearly outlining your goals will help you determine *why* you are investing, deepen your conviction in investment choices, and boost persistence to remain invested during the ups and downs of market cycles. Remember: market declines are a normal part of market patterns. Investing for the mid- to long term and understanding the psychology behind emotion-driven decisions can help you avoid getting caught in the cycle of investor emotions.

THE POWER OF BIASES

Your personal experiences, values, and beliefs influence your financial decisions. Your money memories create your personal biases toward money. These biases are deeply rooted and frequently subconscious. While it is important to consider biases in the context of financial decision-making, I encourage you to think about other areas of your life they could be impacting as well.

By relying too much on a piece of information, you can "anchor" your decision-making. **Anchoring bias** in investing occurs when you are too focused on your original purchase price, historical values, or all-time highs. These can become focal points for your subconscious, causing you to ignore other pertinent information. Make sure that you are giving enough consideration to current conditions and not making decisions based on an anchor point.

Confirmation bias impacts how you gather information, seeking information that supports and confirms your existing beliefs. It influences how you interpret and remember information, limiting your ability to make purely rational decisions. Look to multiple information sources and challenge your own thinking.

Your brain is wired to remember what happened most recently, skewing perception toward short-term thinking. Placing greater emphasis on recent events is called **recency bias**, and it correlates heavily with the cycle of emotions. In terms of investing, recency bias most frequently occurs when investors make decisions based on recent market events, *assuming* those events will continue into the future. Avoid getting caught up in investment trends by making decisions based on your personal risk tolerance and specific investment goals.

Herd mentality bias is a basic human behavior; we like to do what other people are doing. Investors tend to gravitate toward investments because others are making them. The fear of missing out on growth that others are participating in drives your herd instinct. This can result in investments becoming overinflated in price. They can grow only so big before bursting and triggering steep investment losses. The simplest way to avoid herd mentality is to make investing decisions based on your individual circumstances, independently of others.

We tend to place a higher value on things that we own, increasing our fear of losing them. **Loss-aversion bias** is a strong emotion; it explains why we are twice[26] as upset about losing $100 as we are excited about gaining $100. When it comes to investing, we frequently become so focused on the fear of loss that we can miss out on the opportunity for gains. Having a long-term mindset and understanding your comfort with risk will help you stay focused on pursuing your investment goals.

Investors can potentially find these biases to be the biggest hurdles to successful investing. Recognizing your money mindset and natural biases is an important part of eliminating emotions from investment decision-making. Learn key investment concepts and try to understand the source of any fears you have about investing. Stay focused on the goals you set, and when in doubt, slow down to ensure you are making informed, rational decisions rather than reactive, emotional decisions.

TAKE ACTION!

Remember, investing isn't simply about the pursuit of wealth; it's about finding a balance in life. Knowledge is power, and you now have the power to take control of your financial future. With studies showing that women get better returns than men,[27] **ENVISION** how investing can support your goals.

E   **EMPOWER** yourself by acknowledging any fears and biases.

N   **NARROW** your focus by using the timeline of your goals to drive your investment strategy.

V   **VALIDATE** that your personal benchmark is realistic and in alignment with your risk profile and asset allocation.

I   **IMPLEMENT** your investment strategy; start early, and be consistent.

S   **SHARE** your goals with others to build your confidence in investing.

I   **INCENTIVIZE** by celebrating when you are on track for your goals.

O   **OVERSEE** your investments, monitoring every six months to start and at least annually after. Rebalance as needed.

N   **NAVIGATE** life by adjusting your investment strategy over time as your timeline, goals, and circumstances change.

PART II

NAVIGATING LIFE

December

Just like you, Elle, Collins, and Jade have discovered the role psychology plays in their relationships with money and recognize the impact that has on their money mindset. With a better understanding of themselves and the fundamentals of financial planning, they have made commitments to improving their financial lives. Having each defined their vision of financial empowerment, these visions will serve as the driving force behind their intentions. While their visions for the future are as different as they are, Elle, Collins, and Jade are committed to supporting each other on their empowerment journeys.

In the decades that follow, our investors will experience much together. They will bolster their savings, buy and sell homes, change jobs and start new businesses, find new purpose in retirement, and even cope with losing loved ones. We will watch these women experience life—and the evolution of their financial confidence—along the way.

Before we discover what life has in store for each of them, let's revisit where we left Elle, Collins, and Jade in their pursuit of financial empowerment.

ELLE

After analyzing her money memories, Elle realizes that her proclivity for safety has prevented her from making the most of her savings. She recognizes that there are steps she can take beyond simply saving to make progress toward her goals of paying for Ava's education, buying a home, and retiring someday. Elle vows not to let fear lead her financial decisions and is motivated to

- think longer term and look at borrowing options from a more logical, rather than an emotional, perspective;

- leverage her retirement and education savings by making investments that will move her toward her goals more quickly; and

- ensure proper protection is in place to take care of her and ultimately Ava if the unexpected were to occur.

Elle is grateful for the community she has in Jade and Collins to support her as she makes significant financial moves, giving her the confidence to let go of fears that have been holding her back.

COLLINS

As unconcerned as she can sometimes be, Collins acknowledges that she needs to have a better understanding of what it takes for her household to run and to become an active participant in the financial aspects of her own life. Despite her apprehension, Collins knows that if she does not take control of her finances, she could be putting her entire family at risk. Collins resolves to

- understand the balance of her family's income, expenses, assets, and liabilities;

- minimize her credit card debt, becoming a more responsible spender;

- establish SMART short-, mid-, and long-term goals for her family; and

- review insurance and estate planning to ensure the family is properly protected for life's what-ifs.

Collins longs to keep her "ignorance is bliss" attitude but cannot help but be a little excited at the prospect of empowering herself and taking part in her finances.

JADE

Jade has enjoyed exploring financial planning with Elle and Collins. She appreciates that it is about more than just money—it is about planning for a lifestyle that she wants to live. She thought she had a comprehensive plan but has learned that she has more to do and is ready to take action. Jade strives to

- implement SMART criteria for her investment property and retirement goals;
- execute protection planning for her nontraditional relationship with Logan;
- focus on career advancement for her remaining working years, and;
- clearly define her goals beyond retirement—living a life filled with passion and purpose.

Jade recognizes that she may not be as on track with her goals as she thought, but she is confident that she can identify the steps necessary for her to find financial empowerment.

CHAPTER SIX

REALIZING DREAMS

Education, Real Estate, and Estate Planning

As Elle, Jade, and Collins enter their forties, they continue to feel more established in all aspects of their lives and think more seriously about the goals they set for their financial futures. In the two years since our investors committed to a more active role in their financial lives, they have made progress on some goals, and life has interjected itself ahead of others, as it often does.

ELLE

ELLE'S SHORT-TERM GOAL: BUY HER FIRST HOME

For Elle purchasing a home is at the core of her aspiration for security for her family. As it is for many of us, it could be her biggest financial asset. Feeling empowered to take greater control of her financial life, she wants to achieve this foundational goal as soon as possible.

How She'll Do It

To put herself in a strong borrowing position, Elle has been working to boost her credit score. She has been using her credit card for small everyday purchases and pays it off in full each month. Elle's credit score has gone from practically nonexistent to 700! Ever wanting to improve, Elle wants to increase her score to 720. A higher credit score can mean thousands of dollars in savings on interest over the lifetime of her loan.

As Elle continues to boost her credit score and savings, she is ready to better understand the process of qualifying for a mortgage. Elle meets with a mortgage broker, Sara, to explore her options. Sara walks her through mortgage types and her debt-to-income (DTI) ratio.

While Elle has come a long way with her feelings toward debt, she is still uneasy about overextending, knowing there are always ongoing maintenance and repairs, as well as unexpected expenses, that come with homeownership. Elle will target a conservative DTI ratio of 20 percent[28] of her gross income. After receiving a raise and cost of living adjustments, Elle's before-tax monthly income is currently $7,500, making her target monthly debt payment $1,500. Since her credit card is her only debt and she pays it off each month, she is comfortable budgeting $1,500 for her mortgage payment.

> **EMPOWER TIP:** Mortgage companies may allow for your debt-to-income ratio to be as high as 50 percent. However, when running your numbers, be mindful of your 50/20/30 targets when determining what *you* are comfortable with.

Next, Elle and Sara go over some of the additional costs of financing a home: interest, taxes, and insurance. Sara explains that there is an extra insurance cost for loans that have loan-to-value ratios greater than 80 percent. For private loans this is private mortgage insurance (PMI), and for FHA loans it is FHA mortgage insurance. Sara helps her understand these additional costs, as well as how they differ. It can be difficult to afford a 20 percent down payment, especially for first-time homeowners. The biggest difference Elle observes is that PMI falls off as soon as the target ratio is hit, while FHA insurance remains part of the loan for a set period of time, even if the target ratio is achieved.

Fast-forward four years down the road, and Elle is ready to fulfill her vision-board dream by making an offer on her first home. The time Elle spent becoming educated on financing options allows her to feel confident and informed when she makes an offer on a cozy two-bedroom, one-bathroom ranch-style home in the same neighborhood where she and Ava have been living. Fortunately, the hot real estate market in the area will cool off, and Elle will find a home listed for less than she expected, at $325,000.

If Elle borrows more than $260,000 to finance her home purchase, she will have extra premium payments to cover the increased risk associated with a high loan-to-value ratio. Wanting to eliminate the need for extra insurance costs, Elle will look at her finances to see whether she can afford $65,000 as her down payment.

After going through the original 50/20/30 exercise, Elle realized that she was not on track to achieve her goal of purchasing a home. In an effort to get on track, she narrowed her focus and revisited her savings balances as well as monthly saving targets. Feeling secure having one year's worth of expenses in emergency savings, Elle shifted $300 of her monthly savings into her home-purchase account. Those monthly contributions, along with six years of saving annual bonuses, will result in Elle having $60,000 earmarked for her down payment. Because she falls just $5,000 short, Elle will temporarily borrow the funds from her emergency savings. While it was not part of her plan and is out of character, Elle will stretch to get her and Ava into a home of their own before Ava starts her formative high school years. Having worked hard to maintain a high monthly savings rate and substantial emergency savings will put Elle in a position to have options.

Elle's mortgage payment will be the same amount she was paying in rent, $1,450, allowing her to continue her current savings rate and put $300 a month back into her emergency savings account. This set metric, along with additional money from picking up extra instructor classes when she can and her annual bonus, will help rebuild her savings within one year after her home purchase. Knowing her spending and savings ratio will create confidence in her ability to afford the monthly payments and have a plan to build back her savings. The pride and confidence that will come from owning a home that she and Ava can call their own will positively reinforce her decision and sense of financial empowerment.

ELLE'S MIDTERM GOAL: PUT AVA THROUGH COLLEGE

Like all mothers Elle wants to support Ava's dreams, including giving her the opportunity to attend college. Not knowing where Ava will ultimately decide to go, Elle defaulted to saving for in-state public university tuition and settled on $40,000 as her savings target for Ava's undergraduate degree.

How She'll Do It
Elle has been saving for this goal since Ava was born. For eight years Elle put Ava's savings into a certificate of deposit, or CD, that earned

2 percent interest. For Elle's savings style, the safety of investing in a CD seemed logical. However, a downside to saving for college with CDs rather than using other investment tools is that the rate of return on CDs is capped at the stated interest rate.

After our investors' conversation about investing in chapter 5, Elle investigated investment options for Ava's college savings. Her research led her to 529 plans, where Elle narrowed her focus to prepaid tuition plans and education savings plans.

A **prepaid tuition plan** would allow her to pay for future college tuition at current tuition rates. She could purchase units at set installments based on Ava's age, with installment amounts increasing as Ava gets older. The plan would be guaranteed by the state, and the funds could be used to cover eligible costs such as tuition and fees. While it would help her lock in tuition costs today, there are also limitations for her to consider. The funds must be used for qualified expenses only and cannot be used for room and board. Additional restrictions include age, grade, and residency requirements. While the funds can be used for out-of-state colleges and universities, the guaranteed value would be lost.

In addition to prepaid tuition, she considered an **education savings plan**. Unlike the prepaid tuition, the education savings plan allows you to make contributions into a separate investment with funds accumulating tax-free when used for higher education costs, including tuition, room and board, fees, books, and other supplies. Elle would be responsible for making investment decisions and managing future distributions. There is no lock-in of current costs or state guarantee, and there are also no age, residency, or enrollment-period limitations.

While Elle was initially drawn to the guarantees of the prepaid tuition plan, she liked the flexibility that the education savings plan would create for Ava. Financial empowerment is about creating choices, and she wanted to help create that power of choice for her daughter.

EMPOWER TIP: Some states offer tax benefits for 529 contributions. The benefits vary from state to state, making it important to understand the state tax benefits for the plan you choose.

Elle invested the $10,300 she had saved in a 529 education savings plan for Ava. She allocated the funds to an aged-based mutual fund portfolio, which automatically rebalances, adjusting the risk over time as Ava nears college age. Once again, taking action was not an easy decision, as safety has been Elle's default financial philosophy. However, she realized that a CD would not leverage her dollars as much as the combined benefits of the investment and tax-free earnings that a 529 savings plan creates. She made the decision that would help her make the most progress toward her goal and benefit Ava the most.

When she started the 529 savings account, Elle had a ten-year horizon to reach her goal. Now, two years later, she has a balance of just under $14,000 and estimates she will have $32,500 when Ava is headed to college (assuming her 5 percent personal benchmark target). That's $9,000 more than her original approach of rolling over the 2 percent CD every year, plus the tax benefits on the earnings. Having a projected balance for when Ava will start school helps Elle anticipate the shortfall. Once Elle rebuilds her emergency savings, she resolves to allocate an extra $300 per month to Ava's college savings to make it achievable.

ELLE'S LONG-TERM GOAL: RETIREMENT

Elle has also been contributing to her Roth IRA every month since she was twenty-five. She is proud of how hard she has worked to contribute the maximum annual amount, but she has always questioned whether she is saving enough. Just like with Ava's education savings, Elle realizes she could and should be doing more with her retirement savings. Investing her savings, along with her monthly contributions, will leverage the money so it will be worth more in thirty years, when she plans to retire.

How She'll Do It

Two years ago Elle invested the $104,000 in her Roth IRA in target-date mutual funds that manage asset allocation to adjust over time as the specified year grows closer. Elle likes the approach of using a target-date fund because she can pick a date that aligns with her anticipated retirement date as well as dates ahead of that to further reduce some of her risk. Elle split the money into three target-date funds, each spaced ten years apart. While she remains nervous about investing the money, she will monitor her accounts every six months, rebalance annually, and increase her contributions when the limits increase.

Today her account balance is over $127,000, $6,800 more than if she had left it at the bank. Assuming Elle continues to make a $500 monthly contribution and earns her personal benchmark target of 5 percent, her Roth IRA will be worth $950,000 at age seventy. Elle will continue to become more confident as an investor and make peace with the fact that the account balance will not always go up. Monitoring the accounts regularly will help show that the upside of investing balances the risk. With thirty years until retirement, she reminds herself that it's a long-term investment and that she should think in decades, not quarters.

COLLINS

COLLINS'S SHORT-TERM GOAL: CREATE A HOUSEHOLD BUDGET AND STICK TO IT

After her conversations with Elle and Jade, Collins sought to have a better understanding of her family's finances. She committed to pay down her credit card balances, decrease her lifestyle spending by 10 percent, and, ultimately, make and stick to a budget. Acknowledging that she does not know where all their money is spent, she hopes that taking a closer look at their day-to-day expenses will inspire her to be more mindful of her spending.

How She Did It

Collins's first step was working with James to go through their finances. As soon as he opened his spreadsheet, Collins became disinterested. His system did not work for her; it's just not the way she thinks. On her own, she set up an online budgeting tool. It took some time to go through all their income and expenses and create a budget. She allocated their spending into the categories she estimated in chapter 2: everyday essentials, goals and reserves, and lifestyle. This allows her to monitor their actual versus target spending. By setting up the budget tracker, she was able to demonstrate that even though she was spending less, she was falling short of her goal to cut lifestyle spending by 10 percent. She continues to monitor their spending monthly but struggles to identify the areas where they can make bigger strides in reducing expenses.

In an effort to rein in her spending, Collins reduced the number of credit cards she uses. To eliminate the temptation of using her multitude of cards, she cut them up, and once the final bill was paid, closed the accounts she no longer planned to use. While this may have helped Collins reduce her spending, she discovered an unintended consequence of closing her credit cards. Her available credit limit decreased, which increased her credit utilization rate. Narrowing down the number of credit cards she uses has made it easier for her to track her spending, as well as the overall credit balance she maintains. Knowing how much credit card debt she is carrying has enabled her to achieve her goal of better managing her overall debt.

> **EMPOWER TIP:** Rather than closing credit cards with no annual fee, consider storing them with your essential documents. This will help you avoid temptation without impacting your credit utilization.

COLLINS'S MIDTERM GOAL: BUY A FAMILY VACATION HOME

In further reflecting on what she wants from financial empowerment, Collins put time with her family at the top of her list. Over the years Collins and James have talked about a vacation property, but they can't agree on a vacation destination, let alone where they would want a house. As we saw with their approaches to budgeting, they frequently do not start out on the same page when it comes to money. Collins wants to work with James to narrow their focus, set shared goals, and take action together.

KNOW YOURSELF AND YOUR PARTNER. UNDERSTAND EACH OTHER'S MONEY MEMORIES AND WHERE YOUR PARTNER IS COMING FROM.

How She'll Do It

It can be challenging to have difficult conversations with a partner, especially about money. As we learned when exploring money memories, money means different things to everyone. You may view money as a means for providing security, while your partner views it as a tool for creating opportunity. Or you may be a spender by nature, while your partner focuses on saving. If your ideals do not match, it can cause tension and even conflict. Collins finds the following tips to be helpful in her conversations with James:

Know yourself and your partner. Understand each other's money memories and where your partner is coming from.

Define and agree on your roles. What role have you been playing in your financial life? Are you comfortable with that? Do you agree on each other's spending? How are you managing your spending? Identify where you can compromise.

Make it an official event; treat it like a meeting at work. Be prepared and ready to listen. To start, you can discuss all finance, household, and family items at a predetermined time each week.

Collins and James find that having a structured approach to discussing their finances makes their conversations easier. Together they do the following:

- Agree that James will continue to be the one to manage the household finances, but he will make sure all their accounts feed into Collins's online budgeting tool so that she can more efficiently understand their finances.

- Work on spending within the 50/20/30 framework.

- Identify a location for a potential vacation home and set SMART criteria for their down payment.

- Set a target retirement age of sixty-five for James.

Taking the time to have these discussions and be on the same page enables Collins to become more involved and feel more confident about their current and future financial picture.

LONG-TERM GOAL: PLANNING FOR RETIREMENT

Once Collins cracks open the conversation about finances with James, she finds that it is a fairly straightforward discussion. Together they work to validate their ability to achieve the goal of James retiring at age sixty-five. With only James saving for retirement, Collins wants to make sure that he is saving sufficiently for them both.

How She'll Do It

In reviewing James's retirement savings, they confirm that James contributes 5 percent of his $300,000 salary to his 401(k), totaling $15,000 per year. His employer matches 50 percent of every dollar he contributes, resulting in a total combined contribution of $22,500 per year.

With a current balance of $350,000, continuing the same contribution and match rate and achieving their personal benchmark target of 7 percent, his account balance is projected to be $3,400,000 by age sixty-five.

At first glance, these numbers look great, but the reality is that James and Collins are leaving money on the table. Remember, James's employer matches 50 percent of his contribution up to the maximum annual contribution amount. This means that James could contribute another $4,500 a year, resulting in an additional $2,250 from the employer match.

The additional combined employee and employer contributions equate to $450,000 by the time he retires. The employer match accounts for $150,000 of essentially free money that he is not taking advantage of. Every dollar is going to make a difference in retirement. Collins and James should look to maximize all extra dollars available to them.

> **EMPOWER TIP:** You can and should save for retirement even if you are not working. A spousal IRA will allow you to contribute the maximum annual contribution into an IRA of your own.

JADE

JADE'S SHORT-TERM GOAL: GET LEGAL AFFAIRS IN ORDER

Estate planning had been on Jade's to-do list for years, but she just could not seem to get it checked off. She recognizes its significance given her nontraditional relationship with Logan. Their "mine" and "yours" approach of controlling their own assets has worked well for them, but she has wondered if there are other considerations that she might be overlooking when thinking about the future.

How She Did It

Jade contacted Olivia, an attorney who specializes in estate planning. Over the course of multiple meetings, Olivia guided them through various scenarios and circumstances that could occur and helped them identify how they would want them handled. They found the initial layer of questions to be fairly easy to answer. Who would Jade want to make medical decisions for her if she were unable to make them for herself? Logan. If something happens to Logan, whom does he want to be the beneficiary of his estate? Jade. The more layers of complexity that were added, the more challenging some of the questions became to answer. For instance, if Jade becomes the beneficiary of Logan's assets, does she decide who receives his assets when she passes away? Or what happens if something happens to them both at the same time?

Once they determined how they wanted their plan to be structured, it took another couple of months to complete all the pieces, but Jade and Logan finalized all their documents outlining their wishes. They determined who will make decisions for each other in case of incapacity, how they can provide for one another in case one of them dies, and what will ultimately happen to their assets when they are both gone.

It is a huge relief to have completed their legal planning. As organized and thorough as Jade is, like many of us, she put off dealing with these heavy legal matters because of the difficulty of addressing all life's what-ifs. Having a knowledgeable professional guide them through all the hypothetical scenarios was invaluable. She is relieved to have everything in place and realizes that the worry that comes with not having a plan far exceeds the process, and cost, of getting your affairs in order.

JADE'S MIDTERM GOAL: ADDITIONAL INVESTMENT PROPERTY

Jade's big plan to retire early puts greater emphasis on creating future income sources. The need for this is twofold: (1) income sources such as retirement account distributions and Social Security will not be available to her at her target retirement age, and (2) retiring earlier means that she will have a longer retirement period that needs to be supported. In anticipation of these issues, Jade and Logan set a goal to purchase another rental property to support their long-term goal of retiring early.

How She'll Do It

Because this is an "ours" property, Jade and Logan agree to participate equally in this goal. Working with Elle's mortgage broker, Sara, they will become educated on the process of purchasing an investment property. They will learn that, unlike when it comes to a mortgage on a primary house, 20 percent down is a requirement when financing an investment property.

Jade and Logan will work backward, first determining how much debt they can take on in the form of a mortgage balance and then determining the amount needed for a 20 percent down payment. The DTI ratio exercise that Elle went through will be completed with Sara, factoring in all current income sources and existing debt, including their respective mortgages. While the purpose of the investment property is to produce income, Jade and Logan will elect not to include the anticipated income in their DTI analysis. With aggressive goals to retire early, additional income from the property will be used to accelerate mortgage payments or allocated to their other goals. Adding Logan, at a DTI of 25 percent, to the equation enables them to afford a greater additional monthly payment than what we saw for Jade in chapter 3. Using a monthly mortgage payment of $2,000, they determine a target purchase price of $450,000. Jade will be responsible for $45,000 of the down payment, causing her to take a step back.

In her goal setting, Jade underestimated a target savings amount of $30,000. Over the past two years, she has made slow progress on that goal and now finds that she will need an additional $15,000 on top of that. That's a lot of money! Having just celebrated the final payment on her student loans, she has already started to increase her savings. Knowing that $275 will not be nearly enough, Jade will look to the lifestyle category to cut back on her spending. Recalling the 50/20/30 exercise, she remembers that she was overspending on fitness classes. In addition to her gym membership, she pays for classes at studios all over town. If she decreases the number of studios she visits, she could save an additional $2,000 a year.

Additionally, the thirty-six-month financing period for her recent car purchase will end soon. She was planning to buy a new car, but continuing to drive her car for another few years would create another $450 in available savings. In total, Jade will uncover $10,700 in annual savings:

- $3,300 annual savings from no longer having a student loan payment

- $2,000 annual savings from exclusively attending fitness classes included in her gym membership

- $5,400 annual savings by continuing to drive her current car

Quickly coming up with sources to save over $10,000 will fill Jade with enthusiasm and confidence that she can find a few more spending categories to cut back on. She will set an aggressive savings goal of $15,000 a year for the next three years to reach the $45,000 she needs for her half of the down payment.

With the savings side sorted out, Jade will start to think about the mechanics of investing in a property together. She is accustomed to their current separate approach to owning assets—mine and yours—and will want to understand the most appropriate way for them to go about investing in an "ours" asset.

EMPOWER TIP: While a smart real estate purchase can be a great long-term investment, don't tie up too much of your liquid assets and monthly cash flow. Be mindful of other goals that you may need money to achieve.

JADE'S LONG-TERM GOAL: RETIRE EARLY

Jade has always been focused on having $1 million in retirement savings when she retires. If you asked Jade how she came up with this number, she would say, "You need at least a million dollars before you can retire," doing her best imitation of her father's voice. While that has been her target, she realized in the SMART goal setting that she needs to determine how that is achievable and set savings metrics to project how she will get there.

How She'll Do It

Jade currently has $150,000 in her retirement savings. She contributes $1,000 per month, and her employer matches $400 of her contribution. Assuming her current balance and monthly contributions grow at her personal benchmark target of 6 percent, her account balance at age fifty-five will be $750,000.

Jade's retirement savings is in a qualified retirement account, which means she will not be able to take withdrawals until she is fifty-nine and a half years old. This will allow the money to continue to grow before she begins taking distributions. Assuming the same rate of return and no further contributions, her account balance at age sixty will be just over her goal of $1 million.

While making these projections, Jade sets milestone account

balances to track her progress to every five years:

AGE MILESTONE	TARGET AMOUNT
45	$295,000
50	$490,000
55	$750,000
60	$1,000,000

Going through the exercise of analyzing projections and setting targets will help Jade recognize that she needs to develop a plan to bridge the income gap from age fifty-five to sixty to make her goal of early retirement achievable.

* * *

We see our investors' short-term goals continue to focus on creating strong financial foundations. Achieving their short-term goals has put them in a better position to be in control of their financial future. In the chapters to come, we will observe how life alters the course of their journeys, the necessary adjustments they will make, and how those changes impact their path to financial empowerment.

CHAPTER SEVEN

WORK IT

Passion Project, Workforce Return, and Career Advancement

In the ten years since we last caught up with our investors, much has happened in each of their lives as they close out the decade of their forties. While they continue to make progress toward financial empowerment, we now start to see the impact that major life events can have on their plans.

ELLE ADJUSTS TO LIFE AS AN EMPTY NESTER

The milestone that Elle saved almost two decades for finally arrived: Ava turned eighteen and went off to college. With $43,000 in Ava's education savings, Elle achieved her goal of having enough money to cover tuition at the University of Washington! But both Elle's and Ava's plans took a different turn when Ava was accepted at a small private school on the East Coast with a much higher tuition. While it is not the choice Elle would have made, she admires Ava for setting her sights high and is proud that Ava has achieved her own dream of attending a prestigious university.

With private university costs being higher, Ava, with the help of Elle, looked to student loans to help her cover the difference in tuition. As with the approach she took when looking at financing her home, Elle took the time to become educated on the different types of loans available, specifically how they were structured during the borrowing and repayment period. She then helped Ava decide which loan structure she was most comfortable with, knowing that she will need to manage payments after she finishes college and starts her career.

As it is for many mothers, sending her daughter off to college was a huge milestone for Elle. With Ava gone Elle now finds that she has more time to focus on herself. Elle has spent time reflecting on her life and what she wants the next chapter to look like. In addition to assessing existing priorities and considering new goals, she is ready to start dating with hopes of finding a partner to share her life with.

SHORT-TERM GOAL: REVISIT THE 50/20/30 FRAMEWORK

Elle anticipated both her savings and expenses would be impacted when she became an empty nester. While she no longer has the expense of another individual in the house, she has significantly higher travel costs. Whether she's flying to visit Ava at school or Ava is coming home for summers and holidays, there has been a lot of cross-country travel. Committed to being intentional with her savings, Elle reevaluated her spending and saving.

How She Did It
Elle increased her monthly savings to her travel fund to $300 per month, earmarking $3,600 per year for travel. This account functions

differently than her other savings goals. The purpose of this account is to build up value that gets spent on an annual basis, making cash the most appropriate solution. The savings accumulate and are available to fund travel expenses, which depletes the account, and she begins accumulating again. This cycle continues on an ongoing basis, resulting in an account balance that is not intended to grow over time but is readily available to cover travel expenses.

Elle had been contributing $400 per month to Ava's education savings. For now she has decided to put $300 into a separate savings account for Ava. She knows that Ava will have unexpected expenses, and she wants to be able to help when those instances occur. Now that Elle is fifty, she can take advantage of the **catch-up contributions** and has allocated additional savings to her Roth IRA. After a few months, Elle saw her checking account balance continuing to inch up month over month. While she is spending more on her own interests and hobbies, she found that she still has more capacity to save and contemplated how she wants to be intentional with those dollars.

MIDTERM GOAL: SAVING FOR HER OWN BUSINESS

Elle's self-reflection led her down an unforeseen path. Without even realizing it, she began to ponder the idea of starting her own business as a side project. She loves the event-planning aspect of her nonprofit job and thinks it would be fun to plan more events outside of work. She knows that there is a lot to think about and understand, but she is excited about the journey and wants to create a plan to make it happen.

How She'll Do It
As her savings continue to increase, Elle realizes that she is not dependent on all the part-time income from her job as a cycle instructor. When

she revisits her budgeting and saving, she finds that she can save an additional $6,000 a year if she continues to work the same hours.

Elle will allocate the extra $500 a month to a business savings account, setting a goal to have $25,000 in the account before she decreases her part-time work. Based on these metrics, she anticipates it will take four years to reach this savings goal and develop her business plan. As she works on her plan, the passion she has for the business grows from a spark into a full-blown flame. Elle discovers just how driven she is to make this dream a reality.

LONG-TERM GOAL: KEEP PLUGGING AWAY AT RETIREMENT ACCOUNTS

Elle continues to grow more comfortable with investing and watches her retirement account grow more quickly than it used to, positively reinforcing her behavior. She monitors the account quarterly when she receives her statement and rebalances it as needed to keep her allocation in line with a comfortable risk level.

SHE HAS LEARNED TO FIGHT THE URGE TO MOVE THOSE FUNDS TO THE SHORTEST TIME PERIOD, INSTEAD BEING PATIENT AND WAITING FOR THEM TO RECOVER.

How She'll Do It

In good years Elle has seen the longest-term target-date fund increase the most because it has the highest allocation of stocks. At the end of the year, she moves money from that fund into her other two funds to rebalance them. She does this to be sure that she does not end up with too much money in her most aggressive fund, unintentionally increasing the overall risk of her portfolio. In down years she notices the opposite occurs—the longest-term fund decreases the most. She has come to expect this, knowing that fund has the highest exposure of stocks and therefore risk. She has learned to fight the urge to move those funds to the shortest time period, instead being patient and waiting for them to recover. She realizes that if she did move the funds, she would decrease the overall risk, and therefore return potential, of her portfolio. Her system works well for her to maintain an appropriate level of risk without getting sucked into the emotional roller coaster of having to decide whether it is the "right time" to move her funds.

Her systematic approach of contributing and investing money two times a month enables her to feel confident in her investment strategy. Rather than putting all the money in at once and worrying whether it is a good time to invest, she invests money systematically on the first and fifteenth of each month to coincide with her paychecks. Dollar-cost averaging allows Elle to purchase more shares when the price per share is down and fewer shares when the price per share is high, resulting in a below-average cost per share over the course of the year, without her having to monitor mutual fund prices.

At the start of each year, Elle checks to see if she is on track for her goal of having $850,000 in her Roth IRA at age seventy. Her balance at the beginning of this year was $246,000. She has now increased her monthly contributions to total $7,000 per year. She uses her personal benchmark target of 5 percent, and her projection at age seventy is $900,000. She is happy to see that she is currently on target but knows that a lot can still happen and will continue to monitor and rebalance as needed.

COLLINS NAVIGATES MAJOR LIFE EVENTS

We never believe the unthinkable will happen until it does, and Collins is no exception. When James had a heart attack a couple of years ago, it threw their world into disarray. Collins thought the worst was behind them when he was released from the hospital, but that was only the first step. What followed was months of doctors and specialists, additional surgeries, and endless physical therapy. James was unable to work for three months and then only part time for the six months that followed. It has been almost two years, and he is just now getting back to physically feeling like himself. In the midst of the health scare, Collins was thrown into many of the roles that James was responsible for in their household, causing progress on other goals to be put on hold.

SHORT-TERM GOAL: TAKING OVER HOUSEHOLD FINANCES

Finding herself in emergency mode, Collins first had to navigate the bureaucracy of health insurance. James was going to see the best doctors and *all* the specialists to ensure that he was getting the finest care, in network or not. Fortunately, they have excellent health insurance coverage, but there were still lots of challenges and obstacles—many of which did not come to light until months later, when the bills started pouring in. Wasn't this covered by insurance? The situation made Collins realize that she was not in tune with the specifics of how these fundamentals worked in their life.

How She Did It
Through James's employer, their family has a high-deductible insurance plan, which meant they paid for medical expenses out of pocket until

they met their deductible. After meeting the family deductible, she was surprised that they still had to pay coinsurance. Coinsurance is the 20 percent of covered medical expenses they were responsible for until they reached their maximum yearly out-of-pocket expense of $13,800. Just when she thought they were done dealing with insurance, she discovered that everything reset in January. A new year meant they had to meet their deductible and pay coinsurance until they reached the maximum out-of-pocket expense all over again.

In addition to medical bills, Collins found their monthly bills had been piling up. James had a system where he reviewed the bills before paying them. Reviewed them for what? Collins wanted to know. James compared the bills to months prior to make sure that everything was in line. For instance, the family cell phone bill had gotten out of control with two teenagers using data. And he always scanned the credit card bills for duplicate or large charges. When he explained it, it made sense, but she was still dumbfounded that he was managing the bills manually in our current age of technology. It was at that moment that she vowed to enroll in autopay and return to using the online budgeting tool that previously helped her manage her spending.

Even as James regained his strength, he remained disinterested in many of the day-to-day duties. Collins continued to manage the household finances and reinstated their weekly household meeting, where they redefine their roles and connect on everything that is going on in their lives. It has been a lot for Collins to navigate, but she has been taking it one step at a time.

After a year of managing the family's financial lives, Collins made a big decision to return to the workforce at the age of forty-nine. A couple of factors impacted her decision. First, the kids are getting older. Hayes, seventeen, and Harper, fifteen, are busy with lives of their own. Frankly, it has been a while since the kids needed Collins around during the day. James's health scare was another major factor that contributed to her decision. Now that she is once again monitoring the monthly cash flow of what comes in and goes out, she realizes how dependent their lifestyle is on his income. If something happened and James was unable to work for an extended period of time—or even harder to imagine, did not survive a health scare—how difficult would it be for her to manage?

When they reviewed their protection ten years prior, James increased his life insurance coverage to $1.5 million, the maximum coverage available through his employer. Realizing that his life insurance would only go so far, Collins didn't want the worry of how she would provide for her family. After some major soul-searching, she decided to see what was out there for a mom with two teenagers who had been out of the workforce for fifteen years.

Collins was pleased to find that many of her connections from her previous life in public relations were willing to meet with her. She spent a couple of months reconnecting and exploring where their careers had taken them. One of her old colleagues had started her own firm and jumped at the opportunity to add Collins to her team. Collins was so excited to get back to her roots that she nearly accepted on the spot, without considering the salary and benefits. Jade reminded her of her previous success in the industry and encouraged her to negotiate for what she felt she was worth. Together they researched salaries in the public relations industry and the position she was applying for. Collins successfully negotiated a higher salary and is now a public relations manager, earning $100,000 a year plus benefits, with flexible hours. The position suits her outgoing personality and skill set while providing greater confidence in her family's financial security.

> **EMPOWER TIP:** A job offer is just that: an offer. Evaluate the offer, consider the full benefits package, and if appropriate, consider negotiating by making a counteroffer.

MIDTERM GOAL: REESTABLISH FINANCIAL GOALS

A major takeaway from James's health scare was that the curveballs life throws you frequently come with a price tag. Collins knows they have investments outside of their retirement accounts that can be accessed, but she does not feel like they have enough liquid emergency savings. She plans to use her new income to build up savings that she can access quickly.

Beyond increasing her sense of security, Collins wants to spend more time with those who are most important to her. As her kids get older and busier, they are finding less and less time to spend together as a family. This topic of prioritizing family time continues to come up in conversation at their weekly household meeting. After some discussion they recommit to their goal of a vacation home that is close enough to the city that the family can easily get to it but far enough away that they can unplug.

How She'll Do It

Collings revisits the **ENVISION** framework when assessing her new goals:

E   **EMPOWER** yourself. The first step is frequently the hardest. Collins took a leap and reentered the workforce, overcoming her own self-limiting beliefs and allowing her to take charge of living the life that she wants to live.

N   **NARROW** your focus. Collins must determine her top priorities: security and the precious time she has with her family.

V   **VALIDATE.** Now that Collins is working, she has her own money that she can allocate toward these goals. She will immediately get to work devising a plan to reach their goals.

I   **IMPLEMENT.** James's accident showed Collins that there is no time like the present. Once she defines her goals, she will take action.

S   **SHARE.** Collins will share her goals with Jade and Elle and continue to have weekly household meetings with James, communicating more consistently about big decisions and their futures.

I   **INCENTIVIZE** yourself. If there is one thing Collins loves, it's a party. First on her agenda for their new vacation property will be to host a weekend with family and friends to celebrate.

O   **OVERSEE** progress. Collins and James will monitor their progress every six months and rebalance their investments annually.

N   **NAVIGATE** life along the way. The past few years have taught Collins the importance of rolling with the punches. She is learning to better defend herself and is ready to swing back or jump out of the way if necessary.

Collins will be amazed to find how easily budgeting and saving now come to her. Something she has fought for so long has become intuitive. Based on the family's everyday essentials, Collins will determine their target accessible savings should be $100,000. With $2,000 a month earmarked from Collins's income, it will take a little over four years for their emergency savings to reach their goal, assuming no additional emergencies come up.

Taking action around their ideal vacation property will also go smoother than expected. After homing in on Cle Elum Lake as a location, they will quickly find a house. Collins and James will purchase a vacation home listed at $625,000. They will sell investments in their nonretirement account for their $125,000 down payment. They will borrow $500,000, resulting in a $2,500-per-month mortgage payment that will be covered with funds from Collins's new job. Collins and James will consider the house to be an investment; the memories their family will create there will last a lifetime.

LONG-TERM GOAL: GET READY TO RETIRE

Now that she has returned to work, Collins enjoys earning her own money and likes the idea of having her own retirement savings. Since she was out of the workforce for more than a decade, she wants to catch up fast.

How She'll Do It

Having met her employer's one-year waiting period for enrollment, Collins begins contributing 12 percent of her annual income. Saving $1,000 a month will help Collins jump-start her retirement savings. One thing that is working against Collins is time. She is currently fifty years old, giving her fifteen to twenty years to save for retirement. This means that she has less time for her dollars to compound and grow than Elle and Jade, who have already been saving for twenty-five years.

Let's compare Collins with Elle to understand the impact time will have on their retirement savings. Elle started putting aside money for retirement at the age of twenty-five. At age sixty-five, she will have contributed $250,000 and could have $665,000 in her retirement savings, assuming her personal benchmark target of 5 percent.

Collins starts saving $1,000 per month at age fifty. It will take her almost until age seventy-one to contribute the same $250,000 as Elle. At that point she would have $550,000 in her retirement savings, assuming her personal benchmark target of 7 percent.

The two women contribute the same total amount. One started early, contributing over a longer period (forty years), while the other starts later and contributes for approximately half the time. Elle's savings emphasize the benefit of starting early. Putting away a small amount each month can make a big difference over time. Even with a lower rate of return, we can still see the impact of additional years of investment earnings. Collins's savings highlight that even with less time to save, it is not too late for her to establish her own meaningful retirement savings.

EMPOWER TIP: Time is a significant variable in investing. The earlier you start investing, the greater your potential growth can be.

JADE ADVANCES TOWARD RETIREMENT

While Collins and Elle are planning to work for another fifteen to twenty years, Jade's retirement age of fifty-five is quickly approaching. With only five years until her target retirement date, Jade is working against the clock to achieve her career and financial goals.

SHORT-TERM GOAL: CAREER ADVANCEMENT

Jade once again finds herself up for a promotion. After being passed over for the same position three years ago, she is determined that this be her time. With strong relationships that run vertically through her organization, she is comfortable and confident with those who hold roles above her and is engaged and inspiring to those who report to her. She is the right person for the job and wants to be in the position long enough to make a lasting impact before she retires.

How She'll Do It

Though Jade previously felt overlooked, her boss has been mentoring her to be a better advocate for herself, something many women tend to shy away from. While being a team player has been critical in her career advancement, Jade's individual accomplishments have not received as much attention as they deserve. For the past three years, Jade has been highlighting her contributions to the company by meeting with her boss to review and

WITH ONLY FIVE YEARS LEFT BEFORE RETIREMENT, JADE WILL WEIGH HER LOYALTY AGAINST HER DESIRE FOR GREATER RECOGNITION AND THE OPPORTUNITY TO ACHIEVE HER CAREER ASPIRATIONS.

document the progress she is making on her career goals. She has continued to develop herself, identifying and honing her strengths as well as improving the skill sets that do not come to her naturally.

Jade will be disappointed when she learns at her annual review that she did not receive the promotion that she has worked so hard for. Her boss advocated for her, but in the end he did not have the final say. Jade will face a difficult decision: Should she look outside her company for the career opportunity she is seeking or end her career in a familiar role? With only five years left before retirement, Jade will weigh her loyalty against her desire for greater recognition and the opportunity to achieve her career aspirations.

MIDTERM GOAL: PREPARING FOR RETIREMENT

While Jade's career goals are largely driven by her own definition of success, the financial aspect of a promotion is also a significant consideration. Additional income would help her make progress toward her goal of paying down as much of her debt as possible before she retires.

How She'll Do It
Managing their debt factored in significantly when she and Logan purchased their "ours" rental six years ago. The purchase price was $450,000, of which they financed $360,000 with a fifteen-year mortgage loan. Without accelerating payments, Jade will be fifty-nine years old when the "ours" rental is paid off. The shorter mortgage term resulted in higher monthly payments (and a higher DTI), but they elected to pay more during their working years, while they have higher incomes. While their monthly payment is higher (almost $950 more than a thirty-year mortgage), the shorter loan period results in saving nearly $140,000 in the long run.[29]

The mortgage on Jade's "mine" rental will be paid off when she is fifty-five years old. This will allow her to net $2,000 a month from the rent to support her living expenses. Once both rental mortgages are fully paid off, she and Logan will have nearly $6,000 per month from rental income. They plan to use the income from the rentals, along with savings, to bridge the gap until they can start receiving income from retirement accounts and Social Security.

Jade will construct a net worth statement to review her current financial picture as she plans for retirement:

Assets

Emergency savings fund: $80,000
Retirement savings account: $525,000
Health savings account: $38,450
"Mine" rental: $425,000
"Ours" rental: $530,000 / 2 = $265,000

Liabilities

"Mine" rental mortgage balance: ($75,000)
"Ours" rental mortgage balance: $265,000 / 2 = ($132,500)

Total net worth: $1,125,950

Jade projected that she would need $490,000 in her retirement account at age fifty to be on track for her retirement goal. While she is ahead of her projection, she will continue to monitor and rebalance annually, adjusting her allocation and investment strategy as her time horizon to accessing the funds continues to get shorter.

Jade recommits to contributing to her emergency savings. Most people find that they want to maintain higher emergency savings in retirement. Once she has less income coming in, an unexpected expense could have a larger impact. Jade's goal is to maintain $150,000 in emergency savings.

Since she will not be eligible for Medicare until she is sixty-five years old, Jade has been diligently saving to cover the cost of health insurance in her early retirement years. Here is a summary of her HSA savings:

- The current balance is $80,000.

- Jade will continue to make the maximum contribution for the next five years—another $18,250—until she retires.

- Jade changes her investment allocation to be more conservative because she plans to access the funds in the midterm. Assuming a 3 percent personal benchmark target, she will have $112,000 to help cover her individual healthcare costs.

The high cost of individual healthcare insurance is an important consideration for Jade. She anticipates depleting her HSA savings to cover her insurance expenses until Medicare coverage begins.

Retiring early can be extremely rewarding, but Jade should be realistic about how much money she will need to live comfortably during retirement. She may find herself living for forty years or more after leaving the workforce.

EMPOWER TIP: Remember to factor inflation into your retirement plans. If you assume a 3 percent rate of inflation, something that costs $100 today will cost more than three times that amount in forty years.

LONG-TERM GOAL: THINKING BEYOND RETIREMENT

Retiring at age fifty-five has been Jade's major goal, and it will continue to be her focus for the next few years. With retirement on the horizon, Jade and Logan are starting to think about what they actually want to *do* during their retirement years.

How She'll Do It

It is common for people to be intensely focused on funding this season of life but not have much of a plan beyond the financial piece. Retirement is quickly approaching, and Jade does not have a clear idea of what her day-to-day life will look like. It is time for her to set personal goals for her retirement years, whether that means traveling, taking up new hobbies, or volunteering in her community. It is important to consider how she will create a retirement filled with **PURPOSE**:

P   **PASSION:** What excites her? She strives to always be curious and try new things.

U   **UNIQUENESS:** What are her strengths? How can she use them to be impactful?

R   **RELATIONSHIPS:** Whom does she want to spend her time with? How will she include those people in her daily life?

P   **PLACES:** Where is she most happy living? She wants to pay more attention to her surroundings.

O   **ORGANIZATIONS:** What groups does she want to be involved with? How can she support them?

S   **SERVICE:** Does she have the desire to be of service and help others?

E   **ENDURANCE:** Will she leave a lasting legacy?

Recognizing that many of these aspects are fulfilled through her work life, Jade will start to consider what new avenues she will find to fill the voids that are created once she leaves the workforce.

* * *

Our investors' confidence continues to flourish, each of them benefiting from having built a strong financial foundation. All three have achieved the short and midterm goals they set in previous chapters and remain engaged in their journey by setting new goals when appropriate or necessary. Life events have uncovered the first signs of freedom of choice, which functions as the core of financial empowerment. In the decades that follow, our investors will experience even greater challenges, discover deeper strength, and uncover renewed purpose in life and their financial journey.

CHAPTER EIGHT

NEW BEGINNINGS

Remarriage, Divorce, and Retirement

Over twenty years have gone by since we were first introduced to our investors. Before our eyes Jade, Collins, and Elle have continued to evolve into strong, accomplished women as they journey to financial empowerment. As they turn the corner into their sixties, we will see them lean on this strength as they find themselves in new roles and continue to adapt to the ever-changing moments of life.

ELLE HAS A NEW HUSBAND AND A NEW BUSINESS

The big news in Elle's life is that she's gotten remarried, tying the knot with a wonderful man, Aiden. After Ava continued to plant roots on the East Coast by starting a family of her own, finding someone to share her life with has breathed new life into Elle. Events by Elle is another major development in her life: she's gotten her part-time event-planning business off the ground. The number of events has been steadily growing, resulting in $60,000 a year in income from her side hustle! She has continued to maintain her primary job but has decreased her hours to part time to allow her to focus more on her business. So much change in her life has caused her to reevaluate her existing financial mindset and goals.

SHORT-TERM GOAL: ORGANIZE FINANCES WITH AIDEN

Getting remarried was a major life step for Elle. She had been single for so long after her first marriage ended, focusing on being a great mom and supporting Ava's dreams and her own financially. It was hard for her to open her life to someone else, but when Aiden came along, she knew that she was ready. At sixty she knows what she wants and is more confident in herself and her finances.

How She Did It

It was important to Elle that Aiden be fiscally responsible and for her to maintain control of her own finances. She was initially nervous to tell him some of the struggles she has had over the years but happily discovered that their values aligned, as well as their philosophies about money.

Aiden took the time to understand where Elle was coming from and worked together to come up with a strategy that allows them to maintain separate funds and easily share expenses when desired. With both having a propensity to save, they found they each had ample money in the bank and decided to set up a joint checking account, which they contribute to equally. Shared expenses are paid from their joint account while they continue to use their personal accounts for individual goals, savings, and expenses.

Where they would live was another major decision that needed to be made. Elle's home is very important to her, representing many years of hard work, diligent savings, and independence. Wanting to stay in her house, Aiden sold his home and moved in with Elle. In their legal planning, Elle retained full ownership of her home, and the proceeds of Aiden's house sale were titled as his separate property.

Elle and Aiden prioritized sharing each other's goals. Aiden had always been drawn to strong women and enthusiastically supported Elle's business goals. Wanting to support her in any way that he can, Aiden plans to continue working as long as she remains passionate about her business. While Elle started saving earlier for retirement, Aiden had been increasing his savings since his youngest son graduated from college and he no longer had tuition expenses. If he continues working until age seventy, he will be on target for roughly the same amount as Elle has, leaving them both feeling comfortable with their own financial empowerment and each other's.

Elle and Aiden also reviewed their insurance coverage. Employee benefits, particularly health insurance, should always be reviewed after a major life event. Elle is now being covered under Aiden's health insurance, making it an "ours" expense. Moving to Aiden's insurance gave Elle the option to reduce her employment hours to part time without having to pay for individual health insurance.

EMPOWER TIP: Explore each partner's employer health coverage to maximize benefits and, in some cases, decrease costs. Marriage is a qualifying event that allows you to make a change in coverage without having to wait until open enrollment.

Having determined how they wanted to structure their assets, Elle and Aiden took the necessary legal steps to protect their planning. Elle and Aiden contacted Jade's estate planning attorney, Olivia, to help them formalize and implement their plan. Olivia was extremely helpful in making sure they had considered the ramifications of their decisions and walked them through options that would enable them to have more in their "ours" category. Their goal is to make assets available to the surviving spouse during their lifetime but still earmarked for their own children. For blended families like Elle and Aiden's, certain types of trusts, such as credit shelter trusts (CSTs), bypass trusts, and qualified terminable interest property (QTIP) trusts, can provide a spouse with financial support while maintaining assets for the ultimate beneficiaries, their own children.

After finalizing the documents with Olivia, Elle wanted Ava to know how they structured their estate plans and where to locate the legal documents. During one of Ava's visits, Elle asked her to sit down to discuss the plans they had put in place. While it is never easy to have such conversations, it is important. Not only did Ava learn of her mother's wishes, but it marked one of the first times she had heard her mom talking about money from a position of strength rather than fear. Ava and Elle left the conversation with a sense of relief, both knowing that the other would be taken care of.

MIDTERM GOAL: WRITE A BUSINESS PLAN THAT COVERS THE NEXT FIVE TO TEN YEARS

Ava has continued to notice a transformation in Elle's confidence, most notably in her decision to launch her own event-planning business. While Elle claims that it was Aiden's support and encouragement that enabled her to take the leap, Ava knows it is more than that.

Striking out with her own business is just the latest way Elle is modeling confidence for her daughter.

In addition to Aiden, Jade has been a major champion of Elle's business. While Elle has seen her business as something primarily for enjoyment—it is a bonus that she earns some extra money—Jade encourages her to take it seriously as a business. It is just the push she needed. As a result of Jade's advice, Elle reevaluates her business plan.

HER BUSINESS PLAN PROVIDES STRUCTURE TO THINK THROUGH CRITICAL ASPECTS AND OUTLINE HOW SHE WILL GROW HER BUSINESS.

How She'll Do It

As the blueprint for her business, her business plan provides structure to think through critical aspects and outline how she will grow her business.

Elle will start by answering the following questions:

- Which new ideas should she prioritize, and which should she put aside?

- Who are her best, most profitable customers—her "target market"?

- What gives her a true and sustainable competitive advantage?

- What are realistic expectations for future cash flow and capital needs?

- What are her succession plan and options to exit the business?

Besides wanting her business to thrive and provide income until she decides to retire, part of Elle's long-term business plan is to build it up as an asset that she can potentially sell, adding to her savings for retirement.

LONG-TERM GOAL: GETTING READY TO RETIRE

While Elle hopes to be able to realize equity from the sale of the business someday, she knows that she needs to continue to be diligent about saving for retirement outside of her business. Now that she is married, their joint income exceeds the Roth IRA income limits, making Elle ineligible to continue making contributions. Elle needs to reassess her retirement savings strategy in light of her new financial circumstances.

How She'll Do It

At her accountant's recommendation, Elle will establish a simplified employee pension, or SEP, plan. A SEP plan is a type of retirement plan that allows those who are self-employed or small business owners to contribute to traditional IRAs (SEP IRAs) through their business.

Elle can contribute 25 percent of income earned from her event-planning business (up to the annual limit) to her SEP IRA each year. She must also contribute the same percentage to any employees that have worked for the company in three of the last five years. She projects the contributions to her SEP IRA will be $625 per month. The contributions she makes are tax deductible for her business, an additional benefit as her business pays taxes at a higher tax rate than she does as an individual. Elle estimates that over ten years her SEP IRA will have approximately $95,000 in contributions and earnings (assuming her 5 percent personal benchmark target).

While Elle can no longer make new contributions to her Roth IRA, her balance of $545,000 will continue to grow. If we assume her 5 percent personal benchmark return, her balance at her target retirement age is projected to be $900,000. Having started saving in her Roth IRA at an early age will prove to be extremely beneficial to Elle in retirement.

In retirement the amount of income one needs varies widely from person to person. Most commonly, people find that they need to replace between 70 to 85 percent of their income.[30] In determining her retirement income target, Elle reviews her spending and savings in the 50/20/30 framework.

Having always been a high saver, Elle will target replacing 80 percent of her preretirement income, $8,000 per month. At age seventy half of her income need will be covered by her Social Security benefits.[31] Distributions from her retirement accounts will supplement a large portion of her remaining income need. The sources of Elle's retirement income include the following:

- Social Security income of $4,000

- Distributions from her Roth IRA of $2,525 (tax-free)

- Distributions from her SEP IRA of $275

With these projections, she finds that her income will fall short of her monthly target by $1,200. But Elle will not be discouraged. One of the benefits of having her own company is the flexibility it offers. She can continue to run her business part time into retirement, which will enable her to make up for her income shortfall and continue to save. Identifying her shortfall will also help Elle set a sale price for her business if she decides to pursue a sale as an exit strategy. Elle's business will allow her to create options and make decisions, putting her in control of her own future.

COLLINS NAVIGATES DIVORCE

Elle is not the only one of our investors adjusting to changes in marital status. Since we last checked in with Collins, she and James decided to separate. There was no single event that triggered their decision, but over the years they found they had drifted apart. Even though their decision to separate was amicable, it was an emotional and stressful period. Ultimately, she and James decided to divorce, and Collins was stunned to find how difficult the process actually was. Four years later she is still struggling with the emotional toll.

The best advice Collins received was to have her own legal representation. While she and James were able to iron out the terms of their financial settlement without much disagreement, having an advocate to represent her best interests helped minimize her stress and made her feel more confident in the legally binding decisions she was making.

SHORT-TERM GOAL: ADJUST TO A SINGLE-INCOME HOUSEHOLD

As a result of her divorce, Collins became the head of a single-income household that included twenty-four-year-old Hayes and twenty-two-year-old Harper, who had been living at home since they finished college. As she continues to adjust to her new normal, Collins will revisit the steps she initially took decades earlier to understand her household finances.

How She'll Do It

At the time of their divorce, Collins's and James's assets minus liabilities were valued at $4 million. Residing in a community property state means that Collins was entitled to half their net worth. While most of their assets could be easily divided, they had to decide how to handle their real estate holdings. They both agreed that they would sell their vacation home, but Collins was adamant that she wanted to continue living in their house with Hayes and Harper.

Dividing the primary home is often an emotionally fraught part of a divorce, but it is important to consider this critical decision rationally, as a home can be a couple's biggest financial asset. There were several ramifications to Collins electing to maintain ownership of the home as part of the divorce process. First, Collins had to refinance and qualify for a mortgage as a single applicant to retain the mortgage on the house. Second, the home comprised a large part of her settlement, limiting the other assets that she received. Last, there will be a future tax consideration if she sells the house.

In addition to the primary residence, Collins focused on security for the balance of the assets that she received. With the help of her attorney, she prioritized her desire to have ample cash on hand for unexpected life events and a healthy balance of retirement savings to be well positioned for her upcoming retirement years. Here is the breakdown of Collins's postdivorce net worth:

Assets

Emergency savings: $170,000
Retirement savings: $630,000
Primary residence: $1,625,000

Liabilities

Primary residence mortgage balance: ($325,000)

Total net worth: $2,100,000

Note that the sum of the assets she received is slightly more than half of their community net worth because, with the exception of the cash, taxes have not been paid on the other assets.

> **EMPOWER TIP:** Always consider after-tax value when dividing assets, especially when valuing retirement accounts and highly appreciated assets.

Reentering the workforce and having become more involved in her family's financial life helped Collins feel more confident throughout the divorce process. Having her own income was vital for her to feel in control of her financial future. When reassessing her new household 50/20/30 guidelines, she used only her earned income. The divorce settlement included five years of spousal support, but with that income being for only a limited period of time, it was important to her that she did not depend on it for any of her essential everyday expenses. Instead, Collins earmarked those payments to cover the extra costs that came with the kids living at home. Now that she is in her final year of alimony payments, she is grateful for the financial empowerment her own income has created.

Collins's transition to a single-income household will impact not only her current but also her future income. Her new reality means only one income in retirement, igniting a desire to further bolster her savings. Striving to further improve her sense of security, she increased her retirement contribution to $1,250 per month and adds $250 per month to her emergency savings.

Knowing how valuable savings outside of retirement accounts can be in creating options, she is also motivated to establish investment savings. She has been investing $1,000 a month into an after-tax investment account. Unsure of when she could want to access the funds, she has invested them more conservatively, with a personal benchmark of 3 percent a year. She has built up $50,000 in the account and anticipates having $150,000 by the time she retires.

Collins feels confident that she is on track financially, something that she was concerned about in the midst of the divorce. It was hard to see what life would be like on the other side, but after living it for a few years, she is encouraged by the progress she is making.

MIDTERM GOAL: DOWNSIZING

Divorce is an emotional, life-changing process, making it difficult to keep a clear head when making the important financial decisions that come along with it. There are many common financial missteps that happen during a divorce, including underestimating tax implications, debt division, inflation, and investment returns.

These mistakes can easily be avoided with the guidance of a divorce attorney. Looking back, Collins thinks she may have been too short sighted in disregarding some of her attorney's advice. She was thinking long term when she elected to forgo splitting their joint investment account in exchange for more retirement assets, but she now admits that she may have been letting her heart do the thinking when it came to the house. Collins has more house than she needs or wants to maintain. While the decision felt right at the time, she now wonders if it is where she wants to continue to live in the future.

How She'll Do It

Hayes and Harper were the main drivers in Collins's decision to keep the house. At the time they were both still living at home but have since started to find their own way. Hayes recently relocated to Portland for a job opportunity, and Harper has a serious girlfriend that she is practically living with. Collins realizes that she was keeping the house more for the kids than herself. She contacts a real estate agent and starts looking for smaller properties that better suit her needs.

Collins plans to use the equity from selling her house to pay cash for her next home, eliminating her mortgage. Collins projects her sales proceeds to be $1.2 million after factoring in closing costs and mortgage payoff. She knows that she will have a tax liability and asks her real estate agent to help her better understand how much she will owe in taxes.

Collins and James purchased the house twenty-eight years ago for $650,000. This is the "cost basis." If Collins sells the house, she will have to pay capital gains taxes on any amount in excess of the cost basis, plus a capital gains exclusion amount of $250,000 ($500,000 if she were still married). The amount that will be excluded from taxes is $900,000, making her capital gain $600,000. Assuming a capital gains tax rate of 20 percent, she will owe $120,000 in taxes. You can see why considering the after-tax value of assets is key in divorce negotiations. Let's carry this through to see how much money Collins will have to purchase a new house.

Net proceeds from sale = $1,500,000

Less mortgage balance = $300,000

Less capital gains taxes = $120,000

Available cash = $1,080,000

At age sixty-two Collins will purchase a gorgeous home in a new housing development geared toward social retirees for $760,000. She will be excited to own a new-construction home (less maintenance!) and to be surrounded by neighbors that are as outgoing and socially active as she is. For possibly the first time in her life, Collins's purchase will come in under her budget. With the remaining money from her house sale, she will add $20,000 to savings and invest $300,000 in her after-tax investment account. Having no mortgage payment and increasing her investment funds will help Collins feel more secure in her financial circumstances as she nears retirement.

LONG-TERM GOAL: REBALANCING FOR RETIREMENT

While Collins and James had targeted retiring at sixty-five, knowing that every additional working year can make a difference, Collins reset her retirement age to sixty-seven. With retirement on the horizon, she wants to ensure that her new circumstances will allow her to meet her retirement goal.

How She'll Do It

Collins received a qualified domestic relations order, or QDRO, as part of her final divorce documents. The QDRO instructed James's retirement plan to transfer $550,000 from his 401(k) into her name, allowing her to add it to her 401(k), based on the terms of their divorce agreement. At the time that she consolidated the funds into her account, she also updated her beneficiaries, removing James and listing Hayes and Harper as equal primary beneficiaries of the account.

> **EMPOWER TIP:** It is crucial to update your beneficiaries after any major life event.

Since then Collins's consolidated 401(k) has continued to grow with her annual addition of $15,000 and achievement of her personal benchmark target of 7 percent. Now, four years later, the current balance in her retirement account is $900,000. At the same contribution and return rates, the balance is projected to be $1.6 million when she reaches retirement.

For retirement Collins targets needing 75 percent of her preretirement income, $9,375 per month. Her monthly income sources in retirement will include the following:

- Social Security: $2,500

- Distributions from IRA: $5,150

- Income from investment account: $1,725

Collins finds that her monthly Social Security benefit of $2,500 will be lower than Elle's for two reasons. One, she plans to start her benefit three years prior to Elle. Two, her benefits will be impacted from the fifteen years she spent out of the workforce when her children were young.

EMPOWER TIP: To be eligible for your own Social Security benefits, you must have worked a minimum of ten years. If you work less than that, you can still be eligible for benefits under your spouse or even ex-spouse.

Downsizing and eliminating her mortgage payment ahead of retirement will contribute greatly to Collins's ability to have options and control her future. It will give her a few years to live with reduced expenses as a trial. If Collins finds that it is difficult to cover her expenses based on her estimated income need, she can consider pushing her retirement date out further. Each year that she continues working will raise her savings, increase her Social Security benefits, and decrease the number of years she will withdraw from her assets.

JADE ADJUSTS HER RETIREMENT PLANS

After a great deal of contemplation, Jade decided to put herself out there and see whether making a job change would allow her to finish her working years on the high note she desired. She was fortunate to find a great opportunity with a new company and enjoyed the role so much that she surprised even herself in deciding to work two years longer than her original goal. Now that she has been retired for three years, Jade finds herself feeling restless and seeking out activities to keep herself busy. In hindsight, she wonders whether retiring early was in fact the right move for her.

> DOWNSIZING AND ELIMINATING HER MORTGAGE PAYMENT AHEAD OF RETIREMENT WILL CONTRIBUTE GREATLY TO COLLINS'S ABILITY TO HAVE OPTIONS AND CONTROL HER FUTURE.

How She Did It

The decision for Jade to change jobs after thirty-two years with the same company was emotionally challenging. No matter what else changed in her life, work had remained a constant. In many ways it provided her with a sense of belonging. Her desire to achieve her career goals before retiring drove her to seek opportunities outside her established comfort zone. Having always excelled at networking, she was a well-respected member of her business community. She discreetly reached out to a few people that she knew from committees and boards and quickly found that if she was interested in making a move, there were a lot of companies out there that would be thrilled to have her. She was in high demand! After countless coffee meetings, multiple interviews, and introspection, she narrowed the pool down to one.

Jade was reinvigorated by the opportunity but remained focused on what she needed to do to achieve her goal of retiring with reduced debts. She negotiated for a salary that would allow her to both grow her savings and accelerate payments on her mortgage. Jade's after-tax income increased by $24,000, giving her an extra $2,000 a month in cash flow.

Jade reached out to Sara, her mortgage broker, and asked how much they would need to accelerate the "ours" rental mortgage payment to pay it off before age fifty-nine. After crunching the numbers, Jade and Logan settled on an additional payment of $1,200 ($600 each) a month, which paid the loan off three years early, when Jade was fifty-six.

Of the remaining $1,400 in extra cash flow, Jade increased her emergency savings rate by $800, leaving an extra $600 a month for lifestyle spending. Jade decided that she was going to use the money to upgrade her car. She had been diligent about sticking to her budget; she deserved to reward herself. She would need a newer car anyway, and she planned to work another three years, allowing her to finance it over thirty-six months and have it paid off just as she departed the workforce.

Those three years flew by, and before she knew it, Jade found that she was nearing fifty-five. After decades of slowly inching closer to her goal, it was now staring her in the face, and she realized that she was not ready to pull the trigger. Everything had gone as planned; she had achieved the financial goals she had set for retirement:

- $795,000 in retirement savings

- $150,000 in savings

- "Mine" rental paid off

- "Ours" rental paid off in less than one year

Jade elected to keep working until they had paid off the "ours" rental; what was one more year? And a year later, still fulfilled by the work that she was doing, she thought to herself, What's another year? Logan astutely saw that this could go on for quite some time, so he suggested they plan a trip to celebrate their retirement. The European vacation she had always dreamed of! Once they jumped into trip planning, it gave Jade something to look forward to and forced her to pick a retirement date. Jade retired on her fifty-seventh birthday, two milestones celebrated with a wonderful party that included all her colleagues, family, and friends.

SHORT-TERM GOAL: FINDING HER PURPOSE IN RETIREMENT

The first few years of retirement have been a whirlwind for Jade. She and Logan spent three months traveling around Europe, a trip that ignited the travel bug for both of them. In the two years that followed, they traveled more than they were home. Jade was so busy discovering all the world has to offer that she did not have time to miss work. Now that they have been home for nine months, she is feeling restless. Jade has always been a woman with a plan, and she finds that she has not quite figured out retirement living.

How She'll Do It

Retirement has been more of a transition than she expected, especially the emotional factors. The loss of roles, routine, prestige, income, and social interaction have left Jade feeling a bit lost. In thinking about how she would like to be intentional with her time, she continues to consider her **PURPOSE**:

P   **PASSION:** Travel and cooking excite Jade and bring her joy. She and Logan should take cooking classes. She'll research culinary cooking tours they could incorporate into their travels.

U   **UNIQUENESS:** While working she excelled at helping businesses grow and remain fiscally responsible. Could she find volunteer opportunities that would allow her to support the business community?

R   **RELATIONSHIPS:** She enjoys being surrounded by those she cares for the most: Logan, Elle, Collins, Harper, and Hayes. How could she spend more time with them?

P   **PLACES:** She has always enjoyed visiting Palm Springs. How can she prioritize spending more time in the desert?

O   **ORGANIZATIONS:** Throughout her career she was an active member of many professional groups, benefiting from the lasting relationships she fostered. What groups should she seek out now?

S   **SERVICE:** She always enjoyed mentoring women during her career. How can she continue to support those relationships?

E   **ENDURANCE:** Is there anything she has done that will carry on after she has left this world? What could that look like?

Like many retirees, Jade still has more questions than answers. She will continue to narrow her focus; identifying the areas to which she wants to direct her energy is a step in the right direction. It will take time to discover what she truly wants, and needs, from this phase of life.

MIDTERM GOAL:
BRIDGE THE INCOME GAP

In addition to struggling with how to meaningfully fill her days, Jade is also having a difficult time adjusting to her change in income. It is not that she does not have sufficient access to money, but she is paying herself, and she prefers being paid by someone else. She worked hard to save her money, and the paradigm shift from saving to spending has been challenging. She knows that she will feel better once she and Logan start receiving Social Security income, but her full retirement age for Social Security is still seven years away.

How She'll Do It

Social Security and Medicare benefits are an important part of her retirement income plan. Jade has been paying FICA, a federal payroll tax for entitlement benefits, her entire working life and will soon be eligible to receive her benefits.

At age sixty-five Jade will be eligible to enroll in Medicare, the federal health insurance program, allowing her to save money on her health insurance premiums and associated expenses. But deciding when to start her Social Security benefits may not be as straightforward.

Elle and Collins plan to start their Social Security benefits when they retire. Retiring before she is eligible for benefits means Jade will not only have a period when she cannot receive benefits but will also have to make a decision about the optimal age for her to start her benefits. Jade will take a closer look at the numbers to better understand how her benefits will differ depending on what age she begins receiving her Social Security benefits:

AGE	BENEFIT AMOUNT	PERCENTAGE OF FULL BENEFITS
62	$2,250	75%
67	$3,000	100%
70	$3,720	124%

With personal work history determining benefit amounts, similar to Collins, Jade knows her benefits will be impacted by the ten years she spent out of the workforce due to her early retirement. Factoring in her other income sources and good health, Jade will plan to start her Social Security income at sixty-seven, when she reaches full retirement age. Her monthly income sources at that time will include the following:

- Rental income: $4,000

- Social Security income: $3,000

- IRA distributions: $1,750

Jade will be encouraged that these income figures meet her goal to replace 70 percent of her income, or $8,750. Jade worked hard to make sure that she entered retirement with no debt, which puts her at the low end of the scale for income replacement.

> **EMPOWER TIP:** For those born after 1960, you will receive 24 percent more if you wait three years and start your benefits at age seventy.

Jade knows that her income needs will increase over time but feels confident knowing that her rental and Social Security income sources will increase as inflation impacts cost of living. She will continue to monitor her retirement investments, balancing her short-term objective of providing income with her long-term objective of continued growth. While Jade feels comfortable with her income strategy once she turns sixty-seven, she remains uneasy about being so dependent on her retirement assets for funding her needs until then. Her current monthly income sources include the following:

- Rental income: $4,000

- IRA distributions: $4,050

- HSA distributions: $700 (private medical insurance premium)

As a result Jade will consider taking a part-time job for the additional security provided by steady income and her yearning to find a meaningful way to fill her days. She will look for a role that will allow her to create her own schedule, work no more than two days a week, and use her unique skill set to make a big impact at a small business. An opportunity will come from an unexpected place, Events by Elle. Working with Elle will allow Jade to use her knowledge and management expertise while enabling Elle to focus on clients and events. Jade will benefit from $1,000 a month in steady income, plus the added satisfaction of spending more time with Elle and helping her grow her business. The perfect setup for both.

LONG-TERM GOAL: PLANNING FOR LATER YEARS

After retiring, Jade has begun to wonder who will care for her if she becomes incapable of caring for herself. With women living on average three years longer than men, there is a high likelihood of her outliving Logan, who is already two years her elder.[32] With no children and as the youngest of her siblings, she anticipates that she would likely seek professional care. Always one to think ahead, she wants to understand the world of long-term care and how she can plan appropriately for the possibility of such an event.

How She'll Do It

When Jade was younger, she thought of long-term care in terms of ending up in a nursing home for the final years of her life. Since then she has learned that a long-term care event can occur at any point in life and that the earlier it occurs, the more detrimental it can be to one's financial circumstances.

Long-term care needs are triggered when you are not able to perform two or more activities that are part of daily routines. These daily physical activities include bathing, dressing, eating, going to the bathroom, getting in and out of a chair, and walking. Beyond physical ability, cognitive impairment may result in a care need as well. Jade notes that many of these functions may naturally become more difficult as one ages, but after James's health scare years earlier, she knows all too well how a medical event can trigger the need for assistance.

From her research Jade finds that someone turning sixty-five years old today has nearly a 70 percent chance of needing help with these activities during the balance of their life.[33] With such a high statistic, Jade delves deeper to understand which long-term care services and support would be available, should she need them.

Care Options

While Jade initially considered the more extreme cases of requiring care, she starts to think about the potential for needing help with cleaning, driving, grocery shopping, and cooking while continuing to live in her home. Family members typically provide this level of care, and it is not immediately obvious who would assist Jade with these minimal in-home activities. **Aging in place** would be feasible as long as she only needed limited assistance, but she will also consider the options available if she no longer wanted to maintain her own home.

> **EMPOWER TIP:** If you're a family member who provides this level of care, consider adult day cares as a resource to supplement and support the care you provide.

A retirement community would enable her to maintain independence, with flexibility for support. She could own a home or condo within a community with centralized services, amenities, and social events. Or she could elect to rent a room or apartment that includes services such as housekeeping, meals, social activities, and transportation. **Independent** or **assisted living** would minimize some of the challenges she would face while aging but offer only limited medical care.

Nursing homes came to mind when Jade originally started thinking about long-term care. These facilities offer twenty-four-hour access to licensed medical care. There are multiple levels of care within these facilities, as not all medical needs require the same level of skill. Jade hopes that she will never require full-time **skilled nursing care**, but she is aware that for many individuals this level of care may be necessary toward the end of their life.

Cost of Care

Just as she finds the spectrum of care to be wide, the cost of care varies greatly as well. Many factors play into the cost of care, largely driven by the duration and level of medical care needed.

At the low end of the cost spectrum, the average cost of adult day care is $1,625 per month. In-home care and assisted living both average around $4,000 per month. At the high end of the cost spectrum, full-time skilled nursing can cost up to $8,500 per month.[34] With the average long-term care event for women lasting 3.7 years,[35] these high costs reinforce Jade's desire to be prepared for the possibility of an unexpected long-term care event.

As we addressed in chapter 4, insurance can be an effective tool to protect your assets when preparing for unexpected large expenses. Long-term care insurance will allow Jade to leverage her premiums into care benefits if she or Logan find themselves in need of qualifying long-term care in the future.

INSURANCE CAN BE AN EFFECTIVE TOOL TO PROTECT YOUR ASSETS WHEN PREPARING FOR UNEXPECTED LARGE EXPENSES.

As they dive deeper into their research, Jade and Logan discover that there are many other factors that could impact the cost of coverage and an array of options to obtain long-term care insurance coverage. Finding the complexities of long-term care insurance difficult to navigate on their own, they will work with a licensed long-term care insurance agent. The agent will help them better understand the options that make sense for their financial circumstance. After educating themselves on the different policies, Logan and Jade will each get their own long-term care policy, creating confidence and strengthening Jade's financial empowerment.

* * *

This period has been one of transition—personal and financial—for our investors. Marriage, divorce, and retirement are some of the biggest transitions of adulthood for those who experience them. Each represents a major change in identity and financial circumstances. The work our investors have put into their financial lives empowered them each to approach these life changes from a position of strength, coming out on the other side with even greater confidence. In the next chapter, we will see how each of our investors embraces her financial empowerment and settles into her retirement years.

CHAPTER NINE

RANGE OF EMOTIONS

Fulfillment, Compassion, and Heartache

Over the previous decades, our investors have continued to solidify their financial foundations as they have worked toward their major goals of retirement. The confidence they have gained has allowed them to create opportunities and in other instances helped them navigate challenges. We will now see how their financial empowerment serves them during emotionally fraught times, enabling them to make decisions, have options, and remain in control of their own futures.

ELLE EXITS HER EVENT-PLANNING BUSINESS

Elle initially viewed her event-planning business as an enjoyable side venture with the added benefit of providing extra income. As the number of events she planned continued to grow, the demands of the business expanded as well. Developing and running her own business came with a lot of risk and uncertainty, but having ownership and control filled Elle with fortitude. With the help of Jade and eventually Collins's daughter, Harper, Events by Elle became the go-to events planner for local businesses. Without realizing it, Elle found herself the owner of a thriving small business.

Many women-led businesses are flexible enterprises, starting out just like Elle's: a single-employee part-time business. More women are choosing to become business owners to have greater control over when, where, and how they work. Just as she built a company on her own terms, Elle was able to shape how she exited the business.

How She Did It

Elle differed from traditional small business owners in two key ways: her business was not her largest asset, and her identity was not completely tied to the business. Many small business owners spend the greater part of their lives building their company to the point that it is successful. They invest *all* their time and money into it, making it difficult to distinguish between themselves and their business. The combined financial and emotional stake makes selling the business one of the most important financial decisions they make.

While Elle was not defined by her business, she was filled with pride and accomplishment for starting it from nothing and growing it into a successful enterprise. The idea of parting with something that was so much a part of her was challenging to grasp, much less plan for. Whether you are a lifetime small business owner or a relatively new entrepreneur, like Elle, it is important to have a plan for exiting your business. Sound planning will ensure that you do not lose your sense of self or leave money on the table by closing your business rather than selling.

At the urging of Jade, Elle determined her aspirations for the business once she no longer planned to be an active owner. It was important to Elle for the business to carry on. Her clients had come to depend on her, and she wanted them to be able to continue to count on the business without disruption. Without an obvious internal successor, she decided to explore selling the business to an outside party. Elle and Jade determined the value of the business, identified opportunities to increase the valuation prior to a transition, and formulated a plan B, grooming Harper to take over the business in case the right buyer never materialized.

As luck would have it, Grace, a competitor interested in purchasing her business, approached Elle. With a small event-planning business of her own, Grace was looking to expand, and Events by Elle was the perfect fit. Acquiring Elle's business would allow Grace to grow her client list, expand her staff (including Harper as a lead planner), and establish new vendor connections, all in a single transaction.

After spending time getting to know Grace and her planning style, Elle and Grace agreed to terms for the purchase of the business. As part of the sales agreement, Elle continued to work with Grace for two years in a transitional period as a salaried employee. This arrangement created continuity for the business and enabled Elle to continue to have earned income until she reached her target retirement age of seventy. Here is a snapshot of Elle's financial picture at the time of her business sale:

Assets

Emergency savings: $75,000

Additional savings: $50,000

Roth IRA: $875,000

SEP IRA: $70,000

Business sale proceeds: $300,000 (after tax)

Primary home: $660,000

Liabilities

Primary home mortgage: ($65,000)

Total net worth: $1,965,000

Selling her business was time consuming and at times emotional. Elle found that outlining what she wanted and needed to achieve ahead of the sale made the process easier. Elle explored multiple scenarios for exiting her business but ultimately knew that Grace was the right person to take over her vision. Finding the perfect match and continuing to work for two years after the sale allowed Elle to ease into the idea of retirement with greater confidence.

ELLE RETIRES

Reflecting on how much she accomplished with her business, even Elle cannot believe all that she achieved. The life she has created for herself is so much more than she ever imagined. She is overcome with gratitude for all that she has and excited for what lies ahead. Having always been focused on first Ava and then her business, Elle finds that she has not thought much about how she and Aiden will spend their golden years.

> **EMPOWER TIP:** Too often, business owners sell their business without any plan for what life looks like after. Whether you are selling in order to retire or are looking for new ventures, have a plan for what you will do in the next chapter of your life.

How She'll Do It

As she ponders the years ahead, she considers the areas of her life that give her **PURPOSE**:

P   **PASSION:** She loves tapping into her creative side and wants to spend more time painting and gardening.

U   **UNIQUENESS:** What are her strengths? How can she use them to be impactful?

R   **RELATIONSHIPS:** Her family is her pride and joy. She wants to spend more time on the East Coast with Ava, whose family has grown to include two daughters.

P   **PLACES:** Work kept her close to Seattle, but she now has the flexibility to live anywhere. She is ready to find her dream home and is open to moving closer to Ava and her granddaughters.

O   **ORGANIZATIONS:** Which groups does she want to be involved with? How can she support them?

S   **SERVICE:** Does she have the desire to continue to be of service and help others?

E   **ENDURANCE:** Elle desires to spend more time with her granddaughters, creating an environment to foster confidence in their ability to achieve their goals.

Elle has identified the answer to many of these questions, but not all. She has shown tremendous growth in recognizing who she is and what she wants, but like all of us, she still has areas with room to grow. Her biggest realization will be how much her purpose is tied to Ava and her family. Realizing her roots no longer belong in Seattle, Elle will earmark the money from the sale of her business to purchase her dream retirement home near Ava. Elle will recognize that she has truly reached financial empowerment; she is in a position to make decisions about what she wants the most from her life. Remember, when we began goal planning decades ago, Elle dreamed of owning her first home—how far she has come!

COLLINS AS A CAREGIVER

It is a position that many women find themselves in at some point in life: caregiver. For Collins that meant, at the age of sixty-three, becoming the primary caregiver for her aging mother, Eleanor. Collins had been helping with minor things before her father passed away, but afterward she realized just how much of the workload he had been carrying. For the first two years, Collins helped Eleanor with bills, grocery shopping, going to the doctor, and other daily tasks. Over time, it became clear that her mother needed more help, and together they had to decide what that looked like.

How She Did It

As Collins began to feel the demand of balancing care on top of work and life, Eleanor started to feel more and more isolated, living alone for the first time in her life. Mother and daughter came up with a solution to help them both, deciding that they should live together.

Having recently settled into her new home, Collins moved Eleanor in with her. It was a great fit for both, each having their own space but the comfort and convenience of being under one roof. They decided that they would hold off on selling Eleanor's home, giving themselves time to go through a lifetime of memories that had accumulated in the fifty years she had lived there.

Living together made looking after Eleanor much easier, but Collins still found that she was torn between demands at work and home. At the age of sixty-five, she decided to reduce her work hours to part time. While the decision was not easy, downsizing her home and becoming eligible for Medicare both decreased her expenses, making part-time work more financially feasible.

MEDICARE

Medicare, the federal health insurance program, helps with the cost of healthcare, but Collins knows all too well that it will not cover all her medical expenses. Having received a glimpse into how Medicare works by overseeing her parents' medical insurance, Collins knew that it was too complex to figure out on her own. Collins depended on a Medicare specialist to understand the program. They started by identifying the major parts of Medicare to determine which coverage she should carry.

Medicare Part A (hospital insurance) helps to pay for inpatient hospital stays, care in a skilled nursing facility following a hospital stay, hospice care, and some home healthcare. **Medicare Part B** (medical insurance) covers certain doctors' services, outpatient care, medical supplies, and preventive services. And **Medicare Part D** (prescription drug coverage) helps cover the cost of prescription drugs.

Collins opted for a **Medicare Part C plan** (Medicare Advantage) which covers all of Part A, Part B, Part D, and additional services such as vision, hearing, dental, and other health expenses. If Collins had elected for Part A and B coverage directly, she would have considered a

Medicare Supplement Insurance plan (Medigap). These plans work alongside Part A and Part B coverage to cover certain cost-sharing expenses, such as copayments, coinsurance, and deductibles, but do not include prescription drug (Part D) coverage.

> **EMPOWER TIP:** Educate yourself and understand the way Medicare will fit into your retirement plans. Remember, insurance is a form of protecting your assets against financial risk, and protection is essential to financial empowerment.

BEING A CAREGIVER

Beyond sorting out the financial implications, Collins focused on getting herself in the proper mindset. This phase of life could last one or two years, or many more. Having found her household meetings with James beneficial, Collins set monthly meetings with her mother, brother, and Harper, all of whom helped with Eleanor's care. This allowed all family members to be involved in the conversation, including Eleanor, as they established her care plan.

Eleanor's care plan has been relatively straightforward, as she is still able to do most things on her own. She does not need full-time care, but that could change at any time. Collins made sure she understood her mother's wishes and reviewed all Eleanor's legal documents, ensuring they support her wishes. After James's heart attack, Collins wanted to plan for the expected and prepare for the unexpected. To make sure she has a clear picture of her mother's current health, financial, and legal circumstances, Collins did the following:

- Inventoried Eleanor's income sources, expenses, and net worth

- Confirmed that her parents did not have long-term care

insurance

- Assessed Eleanor's current health status, medications, and symptoms to monitor from Eleanor's doctor

- Retained copies of Eleanor's will, durable power of attorney, and healthcare directives, which give Collins legal authority to handle financial and healthcare decisions should Eleanor become incapacitated

- Researched home healthcare resources for additional in-home care if needed

- Researched community programs designed specifically for families providing adult care

- Visited assisted living homes and identified a place Eleanor likes if she ends up requiring a higher level of care

Having established a game plan for the present as well as the future gives Collins greater confidence. Eleanor also has a greater sense of well-being, having participated in the conversations about what could possibly come in the future.

THE LOSS OF HER MOTHER

A year and a half after moving in with Collins, Eleanor peacefully passed away. Collins will forever cherish the time she spent caring for her. With her mother's passing, Collins and her brother became responsible for settling her $2.2 million estate as coexecutors. In her will Eleanor listed five organizations for planned giving. Each of the charities received $100,000 donations from her estate. Collins and her brother were equal beneficiaries of the balance of the estate, inheriting $850,000 each.

For Collins the money came with mixed emotions as she recognized the significance it carried. Her parents had worked hard, provided a comfortable life, and consistently saved, and in later years they were diligent about not spending it. Unlike Collins, Eleanor never splurged on herself, always insisting that there were better ways to spend her money. The fact that the money was coming to Collins at a time when she was mourning the loss of her mother added emotional weight. Her mother's death hit her harder than she had expected; not having any living parents resulted in a loss of identity. The parent-child relationship had disappeared, and she was now an orphan. She needed space to grieve and have closure before making any major financial decisions.

How She Did It

To Collins it was a privilege to be the recipient of an inheritance, and she wanted to be mindful of how she used it. Not wanting to be impulsive, she approached it the same way that she learned to think about other significant money decisions, using the ENVISION framework.

AFTER EMPOWERING HERSELF TO TAKE TIME TO GRIEVE, SHE NARROWED HER FOCUS, IDENTIFIED NEW GOALS FOR HER INHERITANCE, AND USED THE 50/20/30 RULE TO VALIDATE AND IMPLEMENT HER PLAN.

After empowering herself to take time to grieve, she narrowed her focus, identified new goals for her inheritance, and used the 50/20/30 rule to validate and implement her plan.

She set aside 50 percent of the inheritance to help cover her essentials. She did not immediately have a need to cover major essentials (like paying off a mortgage or other debt) but decided to earmark and invest the money to help with those future expenses when they arise.

This will ensure that her inheritance has a lasting impact.

- $300,000 to her after-tax investment account

- $125,000 to an asset-based long-term care policy

Twenty percent of the inheritance would go to savings. She revisited her savings plan and decided to allocate additional funds to her emergency savings. Just as we saw Jade wanting to have a larger cushion, as part of her retirement planning, Collins elected to increase her safety net. Beyond building greater security for unanticipated events, she also decided to set aside money for anticipated events. Her children are both getting closer to settling down with their longtime partners, and she set aside money to help with this expensive milestone.

- $120,000 to emergency savings

- $25,000 to savings for Hayes's wedding

- $25,000 to savings for Harper's wedding

Thirty percent of the inheritance was left for the "extra" lifestyle items. Collins had come a long way from the woman we first met. She no longer splurged on shopping sprees or indulged in luxury expenditures any time she pleased. When she reflected on what she could do with the money that would bring her joy, she thought of her children.

Having already earmarked money for their weddings, Collins decided that she would offer to help Hayes and Harper purchase their first homes. Her parents had helped her and James when they bought their first house, and she knew that it would please her parents to help their grandchildren realize such a major milestone.

Collins gifted them each $60,000 in down payment funds, but she did not want to just *give* it to them. She wanted to make sure they understood the significance of such a gift. This created an opportunity for her to have an open conversation with her kids about money. Collins shared her own money memories and lessons that she had learned. She encouraged them to always be intentional with their money, sharing how she benefited from ENVISION goal setting and following the 50/20/30 rule.

Collins used the remaining $135,000 of her inheritance on landscaping, home improvements, a new car, and future travel funds. Her inheritance had a major impact on Collins's net worth. Here is her net worth statement after completing home projects, purchasing a new car, and gifting to her children:

Assets

Primary residence: $780,000

Retirement savings: $1.5 million

After-tax investment account: $750,000

Emergency savings: $300,000

Wedding funds: $50,000

Travel funds: $30,000

Current liabilities: $0

Total net worth: $3,410,000

COLLINS RETIRES

While Collins continued to work part time while caring for Eleanor, she took some time off after her death and decided not to return to work at the age of sixty-seven. Eligible for her full Social Security benefits, she will use that income combined with income from her own investments and newly inherited funds to support her monthly income need of $9,375:

- Social Security: $2,500

- Retirement Savings: $4,375

- After-Tax Investment Account: $2,500

Having already spent two years living off part-time income allowed Collins to ease into the financial transition of retirement. The emotional transition proved to be much harder. On the heels of losing her last living parent, leaving her career magnified Collins's identity crisis. Who was she at this stage of her life? For so many years she had focused on being a loyal and supportive daughter, wife, mother, and employee. So many aspects of the life she had known had changed. While she would continue to play an important role in her children's (and hopefully grandchildren's) lives, she realized that she needed to rediscover herself and her PURPOSE.

JADE MOURNS THE LOSS OF LOGAN

Jade's world was also rocked by a tremendous loss when her longtime partner, Logan, suddenly passed away from a stroke a little over a year ago. At the age of sixty-eight, Jade was shocked to become a widow. The man that she had built and shared her life with for the past forty-three years was gone. How could that be? She felt like she and Logan had only just begun their best years together. Blindsided by the loss, she is unsure what life will be like without him.

How She'll Do It

For Jade, Logan's death was by far the most difficult life event she had ever had to endure. The best advice she received was that there is no right way to mourn such a loss. There are no rules about how she should feel or her timeline for recovery. She was encouraged to take it one day at a time, and the intensity of pain she felt would lessen over time.

Jade now finds that she has good days and bad days. And while the unimaginable pain is slowly diminishing, she still misses Logan *every* day. She misses him more now than she did in the first few months after he was gone. In the beginning there were so many details to take care of and friends and family visiting and checking on her. She kept herself busy, distracted. But as time has gone on, she finds that the flurry of support and help has faded.

Her friendship with Collins and Elle has continued to be ever present, but while they try their best to relate, they cannot understand what she is going through. Having your partner die is different from getting divorced or losing a parent. Jade knows they mean well, but it feels like she has to deal with Logan's death for the most part on her own.

Collins suggests that Jade seek counseling or a support group to cope with her grief. Elle agrees that it would be beneficial to have the support of other people who are dealing with similar circumstances and offers to attend a meeting with her. Taking their advice, Jade visits a couple of different groups before finding one where she feels at home.

Over the course of the next year, Jade will make a tremendous amount of progress in processing her grief. She will reach the point where her good days outnumber the bad. She will still miss Logan more often than not, but now when something small triggers thoughts of him, she will be overcome with smiles instead of tears.

Beyond the emotional challenges, Jade thought that she had prepared for such an event. Together they planned for what would happen should one of them pass away before the other, but she realizes that she did not actually think that it would ever happen. At least not at this stage in her life. Since Logan's passing Jade has had to adjust many aspects of her life, including her finances.

While Jade and Logan kept the majority of their money separate, they always maintained complete transparency. As not only an active participant but frequently the driver of their financial decision-making, Jade had thought she would feel better prepared for dealing with Logan's estate. In reality she found it challenging to execute their planning, struggling with becoming the sole decision maker.

SETTLING LOGAN'S ESTATE

The planning that Jade and Logan had completed allowed Jade to be not only the executor but also the beneficiary of his estate. As an unmarried couple, Jade would have no legal rights to act in this capacity or be the beneficiary of his assets without such legal planning in place. With the help of Olivia, Jade navigated the steps to become the executor relatively easily. It was the actions she needed to take after becoming executor that proved more challenging.

At the time of his passing, Logan's assets roughly equaled Jade's. They had always looked to maintain balance in that regard. Now that she would be the sole owner of all their assets, she wanted to consolidate as many accounts as possible. In her mind she would just add Logan's assets to her accounts, but not all assets were that straightforward.

She was pleased to discover that the assets outside of his retirement accounts received a step up in basis. This meant that the value of his house, individual investment accounts, and his half of the assets they owned jointly were revalued at the date of his death, reflecting his contribution to be the fair market value on that day. This was significant because it eliminated any capital gains taxes that had built up in those assets.

While Jade was pleasantly surprised by the step up in basis, she was disappointed to learn that when it comes to inheriting retirement assets, there are separate rules that apply to nonspouses. Spouses can transfer the funds into their own retirement accounts and treat them as their own retirement savings. Anyone who is not a spouse, such as partners, like Jade, or other beneficiaries of the deceased, cannot combine the funds with their own retirement assets. Jade had the option of taking a lump sum distribution or establishing an inherited IRA for the million dollars in Logan's retirement account.

If she elected to distribute the funds as lump sum, 100 percent would be taxable as ordinary income. Rather than diminish the value of the funds with a large tax burden, she chose the option of an inherited IRA that would allow the funds, and the taxes, to be distributed over a ten-year period.

With such large dollar amounts in motion, Jade decided that she should take a step back and reassess her current plan and goals. The goals that she had were the goals she set with Logan. She now needed to consider what she wanted for her life moving forward.

How She'll Do It
Just as Collins has done with each of her major life changes, Jade will start by revisiting the ENVISION goal-setting process.

Empower
Letting go of the past has proved to be challenging for Jade. The past is Logan; the life she wants to live is with Logan. While she does not want to live in the past, it is hard to move forward and look to the future, which seems filled with uncertainty. She has given herself

time to grieve, not making any major decisions for the first two years following Logan's passing.

Narrow Focus

A self-care getaway to Palm Springs inspires Jade to purchase a second home there. She has always loved the area and likes the idea of being part of a retirement community in a warm and sunny location. For the first time since Logan's passing, Jade finds that she is excited. In many ways it symbolizes a fresh start, a place that is all her own.

Validate

Jade starts by evaluating the changes to her income. Since she inherited all Logan's assets, his Social Security income is the only income source that she lost. The loss of Social Security income can be challenging for couples like Jade and Logan, who receive roughly the same benefit amount, as they see an income source instantly cut in half.

> **EMPOWER TIP:** If a couple is married, the survivor will receive the higher of their own benefit or the deceased's benefit. Consider *total* lifetime benefits for you and your spouse when electing when to begin receiving Social Security benefits.

Over the past two years, Jade found that distributions required to spend down Logan's IRA over the ten years resulted in her having substantially more income than she needs. She could use the additional cash flow to finance her Palm Springs house, but Jade has always prided herself on not having debt in retirement. She could sell a portion of her assets, but she is not sure that she wants to tie up more money in real estate.

She wishes Logan were there to talk through scenarios and help make the decision. But he is no longer here, and she reminds herself that she is fully capable of making this decision on her own. In the end she determines that she is at a point in her life where she wants to simplify. She wants a property that she can personally use but does not want an additional property to maintain and oversee, especially now that she will be going it alone.

Jade resolves to sell one of her real estate properties in Seattle to purchase the home in Palm Springs. With higher income distributions from Logan's retirement account, she no longer depends on the rental income. It's a logical choice for her to replace an investment property with a property for personal use.

Implement

After much soul-searching and consulting her real estate agent and accountant, Jade made the heart-wrenching decision to sell the "ours" house that she and Logan lived in together and downsize into the "mine" rental house she owned before meeting Logan. She always loved her little house, and moving back will be a homecoming of sorts. It is a single-level home with a small front yard and large back patio. No stairs and less yard maintenance will make it easier for her to maintain as she gets older. She will keep the "ours" rental they purchased together as her sole investment property.

Taking action is where Jade shines. Once she makes up her mind, she makes things happen! Jade notifies her "mine" rental tenants that she will not renew their lease for another year. This gives her three months to get the "ours" house ready to sell and enables her to move into what she is now calling her "Seattle" house before the "ours" goes to market. She plans to give herself six months to settle into the

"Seattle" house before she starts looking at properties in Palm Springs. If everything goes smoothly, she hopes to close on a "sunshine" house in the next twelve months.

Share

Jade has always been excited to share her life with those closest to her. When Logan first passed away, she found this harder to do. She did not realize it at first, but over time she noticed that she was sharing less and less. Everyone had well-intended suggestions for how she should be handling things. But everything became too much for her, and she found herself becoming withdrawn. What she really needed was for people to simply listen and support her.

With the help of her therapist, she will work to let her friends back in and implore them to support the decisions she is making. She will look to them to help her find her way in this new chapter of life.

Incentivize

As Jade learns to take life one day at a time, she also learns to embrace the little victories in addition to the larger milestones. Preparing the home she shared with Logan to be sold within three months will be harder than she expected, both physically and emotionally. She will incentivize herself by looking to professionals for the work that is over her head. For the emotional

JADE WILL FIND THAT OPENING HER HOME TO SHARE HER PROGRESS WITH OTHERS IS THE BEST INCENTIVE SHE COULD HAVE.

hurdles, she will host weekly Sunday dinners for family and friends to reminisce over all the great moments shared at the "ours" house. This will help her stay motivated and allow for the closure that is an essential part of moving on from the home.

Jade will find that opening her home to share her progress with others is the best incentive she could have. As she takes on projects to convert her rental house back into the cozy home she originally fell in love with, she will continue her new tradition of Sunday dinners. She will be driven to maximize the space of the "Seattle" house for hosting, both inside and out.

Oversee

Even after all the real estate transactions have closed, there will still be progress to be made and action to take. Jade will continue to monitor her finances as she gets comfortable with her new income and expenses. She will track them monthly to start, wanting to make sure that she is staying on top of all the moving pieces. There will be many changes between the sale and purchase of the properties, and it will take time for her to settle into her new "normal" spending. From that point on, she will monitor annually with her investments.

Jade will revisit her estate planning to make sure that her previous planning accurately reflects her current circumstances and wishes. As the sole beneficiary of Logan's estate, she will want to make sure that her planning reflects any intentions that Logan may have had. Jade will take this responsibility to heart and identify a handful of charities that Logan supported during his life, in addition to causes that she feels passionately about, as recipients of charitable donations in her estate planning.

Navigate

The years following Logan's death will go by quickly as Jade adjusts to the changes in her life. She hopes that there will not be any more unexpected life events, but she remains prepared. Jade will simplify her financial life as much as possible for when someone else must step in to manage her finances. Whether it be old age, a triggering health event, or death, she wants to ensure that she has taken all the steps necessary to leave a clear road map. She will do so by organizing all her critical personal and financial information and documents in a single place and sharing with her personal representative.

* * *

We continue to see our investors transformed by the emotional and financial impact of the events that occur in their lives. The planning that Elle, Collins, and Jade previously completed helped to achieve financial empowerment, reduced the financial impact of life-altering events, and allowed them to focus their energy on the emotional toll of their circumstances. As often happens, self-reflection comes in the years that follow, and we will see our investors discover the purpose they have long been seeking on their journey to financial empowerment.

CHAPTER TEN

FINDING PURPOSE

Family, Community, and Legacy

Our investors have come a long way since they set out for financial empowerment as young women several decades ago. Their friendship has evolved and deepened over the span of sixty years as they have shared incredible growth, tremendous loss, and everything in between. No woman had the exact same journey, but Elle, Collins, and Jade had each other as they traveled their own paths. They always have supported each other in times of sorrow and celebrated each other's happiness, and they always will.

Now, in their later years, our investors are proud of who they are, the lives they live, and all the work they put in to get to this point. The women still meet regularly, now taking turns traveling to see one another once a year. Let's reconnect with Elle, Collins, and Jade to see how their stories ultimately turned out.

ELLE MOVES TO THE EAST COAST

Elle's trajectory is an incredibly inspiring story. When we began, she was a single mother, renting a home for herself and her eight-year-old daughter, Ava. The confidence she gained by realizing her goals of owning a home and supporting her daughter's education empowered her to achieve more than she ever dreamed of. Creating her own business was a major accomplishment, culminating with the sale of Events by Elle, which allowed her to have greater confidence in retirement.

Elle and Aiden relocated to the East Coast to be closer to Elle's daughter, Ava, who now has a successful career and family of her own. Elle's goals have come full circle. She spends her days maintaining the pristine gardens that wrap around her forever home, capturing the beauty in her watercolor paintings, and listening to the laughter of her two granddaughters. Just as she once did for Ava, she contributes monthly to their college savings account, imagining the incredible things these bright young women will someday achieve.

COLLINS FOCUSES ON HERSELF

Collins's story began with her as a stay-at-home mom of two kids whose husband, James, provided for their family of four. She didn't worry—or even think—about her financial circumstances. But her life took a dramatic turn after James had a heart attack and she was forced to take charge of the household finances. This change sparked her desire to return to work, and she found herself restarting her career. Finding her own financial footing was invaluable when Collins and James decided to end their marriage, empowering her to come out even stronger on the other side.

Remaining focused on financial empowerment throughout these difficult times benefited Collins greatly when the time came for her to act as the primary caregiver for her mother. After spending most of her adult life caring for others—first her children, then her husband, and finally her mother—Collins realized that for the first time in her life, she would truly be living for herself.

With a renewed sense of self, Collins came to life, enjoying all the social activities and events available in her new community. Her caregiver predisposition is put to use looking after Harper's two young boys twice a week, which fills her equally with elation and exhaustion. Her propensity to help others has even led her to establish Women, Wealth, and Wine, a club for ladies to openly share and discuss financial matters over wine. Collins has created a safe space for women to learn, grow, and support each other as they take on more active roles in their financial lives, just as Jade and Elle once did for her.

JADE JETS BETWEEN SEATTLE AND PALM SPRINGS

From the beginning Jade's focus was on early retirement. Dedicated and driven, she put all of herself into working hard and advancing her career. When Jade's career advancement stalled, she found a new opportunity that energized her to work longer than planned. Following a successful career, Jade retired at age fifty-seven. While the transition proved to be mentally and emotionally challenging, she is grateful for her decision to retire early, which allowed her to travel and support the growth of Elle's business. Jade shared an enjoyable decade of retirement with her partner, Logan, before her plans were once again adjusted by his sudden passing.

The period that followed was extremely difficult for Jade, as losing a partner or spouse would be for anyone. With support from family, friends, and her bereavement community, she gradually made her way through the grieving process. In an effort to simplify her life, she sold the house they shared together and returned to the home she had long ago lived in before meeting Logan. While Seattle is where her roots live, she has spread her wings and found a fresh start spending winters in Palm Springs, her new home away from home.

A desire to share the lessons that she learned from her loss inspired Jade to form a survivors' grief group in her new Palm Springs community. Having a support group helped her endure the challenge of losing a partner. Supporting others who are experiencing extreme loss is where she finally found the purpose she had long searched for.

* * *

I hope the financial journey our investors took will be helpful as you **ENVISION** your own financial empowerment. If you have not already begun, now is the time to take action! Start by unlocking your money memories and knowing where you are coming from. Once you have a clear picture of your money mindset, craft your personal financial vision statement. Define what financial empowerment means to you— what you want to achieve *and* why it is important to you. Knowing your *why* will serve as your North Star on your journey.

DEFINE WHAT FINANCIAL EMPOWERMENT MEANS TO YOU—WHAT YOU WANT TO ACHIEVE AND WHY IT IS IMPORTANT TO YOU.

After identifying where you want to go, set SMART short-, mid-, and long-term goals. Short-term goals will serve as the foundation for your financial empowerment, allowing you to work toward your mid- and long-term goals over time.

Financial basics like the 50/20/30 framework and proper use of debt will strengthen your foundation. Avoid lifestyle spending and debt, as remaining an attractive borrower is an essential part of any financial journey. At the core of financial empowerment is having options, and borrowing can create opportunities that may not otherwise be feasible.

Protection is a fundamental component of being in control of your financial future. You will find a direct correlation between your sense of security and overall confidence. Prioritize the appropriate layers of protection for your financial circumstances. The more prepared you are, the more strength you will find navigating the uncertainty that comes with unexpected life events.

Establish a strong understanding of financial markets to feel confident leveraging investments for your mid- and long-term goals. Start investing as early as possible, using the time frame of your goals to drive your investment strategy. Avoid getting caught in the cycle of investor emotions. Acknowledge any fear and biases you may have and return to your *why* if you need to reassess your investment strategy.

You now have the knowledge to take control of your financial future. Be confident and patient on your journey. As we saw with our investors, it will take time to realize both financial empowerment and **PURPOSE**. There will be moments where you feel you have lost your way and times that you will need to make changes to your plan. Look for support from those closest to you, just as Elle, Collins, and Jade found support in each other. If you find that you veer off course or struggle to find your path, pause and reevaluate to determine what your next step should be. Know that you've got this, and do not be afraid to ask for help. Financial professionals, like myself, are always available as a friendly resource to support and guide you.

Finally, as you **ENVISION** the life you want, be mindful of your **PURPOSE**. Knowing who you are and the aspects of your life where you give and receive the most are critical to your overall happiness. Financial empowerment will enable you to control your own destiny, but it is up to you to discover your maximum fulfillment along the way. The best is yet to come. Be intentional and enjoy the journey!

ACKNOWLEDGMENTS

As a female in a male-dominated industry, I want to first and foremost thank the women who have cleared a path for me to follow. Thank you to the women who not only create space for other women but who go out of their way to lift other women up. Because of you, new heights are always achievable.

The process of getting an idea from one's head to a book in a reader's hand involves countless people. Thank you to all those who helped me on the creative journey of becoming an author. I have endless gratitude for your patience and knowledge.

Thank you to the friends, family, and clients who trusted me to share pieces of their personal stories. Without the trust and support of such women in my life, this book would not exist. You challenge and inspire me each and every day.

To my family, both at home and in the office, thank you for believing in me and encouraging me to always strive for greatness. It means everything to share this accomplishment with you.

Lindsey McKay is an owner and principal advisor of McKay Wealth Management. She is passionate about educating and supporting individuals and families who have a desire to be an active participant in their financial lives.

Lindsey has spent sixteen years as an advisor and CERTIFIED FINANCIAL PLANNER™ working with clients to bring all aspects of their financial lives together. Lindsey has witnessed the opportunities and obstacles that money can create, observed how emotions can override planning, and cultivated how to help others navigate their own financial circumstances and behaviors.

Her own education and professional career have influenced her financial planning philosophy. Lindsey earned her bachelor's of science in finance from the Stern School of Business at New York University. While attending school, she worked for a boutique venture capital firm and saw firsthand the relationship between risk and reward. After college, time spent on Wall Street created the opportunity to dive into the nuances of financial advising in the finance capital of the world. And most recently she uncovered her entrepreneurial spirit by becoming a second-generation small business owner.

As a member of NextUp, Cetera Advisor Diversity & Inclusion Council, the Estate Planning Council of Seattle, and the Financial Planning Association, Lindsey actively engages in personal and peer growth development.

Lindsey is a travel and food enthusiast living in Ballard, Washington. In her free time, she enjoys running and experiencing the outdoors and finds purpose empowering the leaders of tomorrow as a Girl Scout troop leader.

A THANK YOU GIFT

You may be finished with this book, but I'm not done giving you the tools you need for long-term financial empowerment!

As a companion to the information in this book, you can receive my *Money Mindset Matters* newsletter for women. These monthly emails contain a timely financial message from me, helpful articles about navigating the financial side of expected— and unexpected!— life events, plus invitations to insightful (and fun) virtual events to learn and connect with other women who are seeking the same feeling of protection and prosperity as you. To get all of this delivered to your inbox, you only have to tell me where to send it. And you can do that right here: www.mckaywealth.com/women.

If you want to work one on one with me to increase your financial confidence, you can find information to set up an introductory conversation at the same link above. I'd be honored to help you work toward a more secure financial future.

Whether we end up working together or not, I hope you'll take advantage of these free resources to help you create and protect the lifestyle of your dreams.

- LINDSEY McKAY

EMPOWER & SHARE DISCUSSION

1. Which character's money mindset was most relatable to you—Elle, Collins, or Jade? How do you think you gained this money mindset?

2. If you are in a relationship, how is your partner's money mindset different from yours?

3. What about your money mindset do you want to change, if anything?

4. What kind of lifestyle do you want your money to fund in the next five or ten years? Why is that important to you?

5. What do you think is the biggest challenge standing in the way of your financial empowerment?

6. Have you defined your target spending and saving framework? How does it differ from the 50/20/30 model?

7. Do you worry you're not doing enough with your money? If so, what do you think would make you feel like you were doing enough?

8. How does the protection planning you have in place make you feel?

9. What are some passages that you highlighted or parts that particularly affected you?

10. Have you tried the **ENVISION** Method for making a financial decision yet? If so, how did it work for you?

11. What part of the **ENVISION** Method do you find most challenging to do?

12. Do you know what gives you **PURPOSE**?

13. Are there areas within the **PURPOSE** framework that you want to strengthen? What steps will you take?

14. If you could give one piece of financial advice to your younger self, what would it be?

15. Will what you learned in this book change the way you manage your money? How?

NOTES & DISCLOSURES

1   For a comprehensive review of your personal situation, always consult
    with a tax or legal advisor. Neither Cetera Advisor Networks LLC nor
    any of its representatives may give legal or tax advice.

2   The clients and situations depicted here are hypothetical only and do
    not represent the actual performance of any particular investments
    or strategy. The hypothetical investment results are for illustrative
    purposes only and should not be deemed a representation of past
    or future results. Actual investment results may be more or less than
    those shown. All investing involves risk, including the possible loss of
    principal. This does not represent any specific product [and/or service].
    There is no assurance that any investment strategy will be successful.

3   Mark Murphy, "Neuroscience Explains Why You Need to Write Down
    Your Goals If You Actually Want to Achieve Them," Forbes, April
    15, 2018, https://www.forbes.com/sites/markmurphy/2018/04/15/
    neuroscience-explains-why-you-need-to-write-down-your-goals-if-
    you-actually-want-to-achieve-them/.

4   Maryalene LaPonsie, "How Much Does It Cost to Raise a Child?,"
    US News, September 7, 2021, https://money.usnews.com/money/
    personal-finance/articles/how-much-does-it-cost-to-raise-a-child.

5   Before investing, the investor should consider whether the investor's or beneficiary's home state offers any state tax or other benefits available only from the state's 529 plan.

6   Some IRAs have contribution limitations and tax consequences for early withdrawals. For complete details consult your tax advisor or attorney. Distributions from traditional IRAs and employer-sponsored retirement plans are taxed as ordinary income and, if taken prior to reaching age fifty-nine and a half, may be subject to an additional 10 percent IRS tax penalty. Converting from a traditional IRA to a Roth IRA is a taxable event. A Roth IRA offers tax-free withdrawals on taxable contributions. To qualify for the tax-free and penalty-free withdrawal or earnings, a Roth IRA must be in place for at least five tax years, and the distribution must take place after age fifty-nine and a half or due to death, disability, or a first-time home purchase (up to a $10,000 lifetime maximum). Depending on state law, Roth IRA distributions may be subject to state taxes.

7   These examples are hypothetical only and do not represent the actual performance of any particular investments. Investments in securities do not offer a fixed rate of return. Principal, yield, and/or share price will fluctuate with changes in market conditions, and when sold or redeemed, you may receive more or less than originally invested.

8   Melanie Hanson, "Student Loan Debt Statistics," Education-Data.org, September 27, 2021, https://educationdata.org/student-loan-debt-statistics/.

9   Board of Governors of the Federal Reserve System, "Report on the Economic Well-Being of US Households in 2018–May 2019," Federalreserve.gov, updated January 30, 2020, https://www.federalreserve.gov/publications/2019-economic-well-being-of-us-households-in-2018-student-loans-and-other-education-debt.htm.

10   Rick Popely, "Car Depreciation: How Much It Costs You," Carfax, February 3, 2021, https://www.carfax.com/blog/car-depreciation.

11 Liz Frazier, "Why Women Don't Purchase Enough Life Insurance … and Why They Need More," Forbes, September 19, 2019, https://www.forbes.com/sites/lizfrazierpeck/2019/09/19/why-women-dont-purchase-enough-life-insurance-and-why-they-need-more/.

12 For a comprehensive review of your personal situation, always consult with a tax or legal advisor. Neither Cetera Advisor Networks LLC nor any of its representatives may give legal or tax advice.

13 All investing involves risk, including the possible loss of principal. There is no assurance that any investment strategy will be successful.

14 The Bloomberg Barclays US Aggregate Bond Index, which was originally called the Lehman Aggregate Bond Index, is a broad-based flagship benchmark that measures the investment-grade, US-dollar-denominated, fixed-rate taxable bond market. The index includes treasuries, government-related and corporate-debt securities, MBS (agency fixed-rate and hybrid ARM pass-throughs), and ABS and CMBS (agency and nonagency) debt securities that are rated at least Baa3 by Moody's and BBB- by S&P. Taxable municipals, including Build America Bonds and a small number of foreign bonds traded in US markets, are also included. Eligible bonds must have at least one year until final maturity, but in practice the index holdings have a fluctuating average life of around 8.25 years. This total return index, created in 1986 with history backfilled to January 1, 1976, is unhedged and rebalances monthly.

15 The MSCI All Country World Index is a free-float-adjusted market capitalization–weighted index that is designed to measure the equity market performance of developed and emerging markets. The SMCI ACWI consists of forty-six country indexes comprising twenty-three developed and twenty-three emerging market country indexes. The developed country indexes include Australia, Austria, Belgium, Canada, Denmark, Finland, France, Germany, Hong Kong, Ireland, Israel, Italy, Japan, Netherlands, New Zealand, Norway, Portugal, Singapore, Spain, Sweden, Switzerland, the United Kingdom, and the United States. The emerging market country indexes included are Brazil, Chile, China,

Colombia, Czech Republic, Egypt, Greece, Hungary, India, Indonesia, Korea, Malaysia, Mexico, Peru, Philippines, Poland, Qatar, Russia, South Africa, Taiwan, Thailand, Turkey, and United Arab Emirates.

16 Investors cannot invest directly in indexes. The performance of any index is not indicative of the performance of any investment and does not take into account the effects of inflation and the fees and expenses associated with investing.

17 Additional risks are associated with international investing, such as currency fluctuations, political and economic instability, and differences in accounting standards.

18 Investing in mutual funds is subject to risk and loss of principal. There is no assurance or certainty that any investment strategy will be successful in meeting its objectives.

19 *Investors should consider the investment objectives, risks and charges, and expenses of the funds carefully before investing. The prospectus contains this and other information about the funds. Contact your financial professional to obtain a prospectus, which should be read carefully before investing or sending money.*

20 The target date of a target-date fund may be a useful starting point in selecting a fund, but investors should not rely solely on the date when choosing a fund or deciding to remain invested in one. Investors should consider funds' asset allocation over the whole life of the fund. Often target-date funds invest in other mutual funds, and fees may be charged by both the target-date fund and the underlying mutual funds. The principal value of these funds is not guaranteed at any time, including at the target date.

21 *Exchange-traded funds are sold only by prospectus. Please consider the investment objectives, risks, charges, and expenses carefully before investing. The prospectus containing this and other information about the investment company can be obtained from your financial professional. Be sure to read the prospectus carefully before deciding whether to invest.*

22 Dollar-cost averaging will not guarantee a profit or protect you from loss but may reduce your average cost per share in a fluctuating market.

23 A diversified portfolio does not assure a profit or protect against loss in a declining market.

24 Rebalancing may be a taxable event. Before you take any specific action, be sure to consult with your tax professional.

25 Lance Roberts, "Opinion: Americans Are Still Terrible at Investing, Annual Study Once Again Shows," MarketWatch, October 21, 2017, https://www.marketwatch.com/story/americans-are-still-terrible-at-investing-annual-study-once-again-shows-2017-10-19.

26 Corporate Finance Institute, "What is Loss Aversion?," 2022, https://corporatefinanceinstitute.com/resources/knowledge/trading-investing/loss-aversion/.

27 Fidelity Investments, Fidelity Investments 2021 Women & Investing Study, 2021, https://www.fidelity.com/bin-public/060_www_fidelity_com/documents/about-fidelity/FidelityInvestmentsWomen&Investing Study2021.pdf.

28 Debt-to-income ratio of 20 percent = $1,500 / $7,500.

29 Assumes 4 percent interest rate on both loans.

30 Hank Lobel, Colleen Jaconetti, and Rebecca Cuff, "The Replacement Ratio: Making It Personal," Vanguard Research, April 2019, https://corporate.vanguard.com/content/dam/corp/research/pdf/the-replacement-ratio-making-it-personal-us-isgrr_042019_online.pdf.

31 Social Security Administration, "Learn about Social Security Retirement Benefits," n.d., accessed April 13, 2021, https://www.ssa.gov/benefits/retirement/learn.html.

32 Social Security Administration, "Retirement & Survivors Benefits: Life Expectancy Calculator," n.d., accessed April 13, 2021, https://www.ssa.gov/OACT/population/longevity.html.

33 Richard W. Johnson, "What Is the Lifetime Risk of Needing and Receiving Long-Term Services and Supports?," Office of the Assistant Secretary for Planning and Evaluation, US Department of Health and Human Services, April 3, 2019, https://aspe.hhs.gov/reports/what-lifetime-risk-needing-receiving-long-term-services-supports-0.

34 Genworth, "Cost of Care Survey," accessed October 2021, https://www.genworth.com/aging-and-you/finances/cost-of-care.html.

35 Tara O'Neill Hayes and Sara Kurtovic, "The Ballooning Costs of Long-Term Care," American Action Forum, February 18, 2020, https://www.americanactionforum.org/research/the-ballooning-costs-of-long-term-care.

CPSIA information can be obtained
at www.ICGtesting.com
Printed in the USA
BVHW071235071022
648922BV00005B/962

9 781642 251371